Rhythm and Rhyme

Open Guides to Literature

Series Editor: Graham Martin (Professor of Literature, The Open University)

Titles in the Series

Richard Bradford: *Paradise Lost*
Angus Calder: Byron
Jenni Calder: *Animal Farm* and *1984*
Walford Davies: Dylan Thomas
Roger Day: Larkin
Peter Faulkner: Yeats
Anthony Fothergill: *Heart of Darkness*
P. N. Furbank: Pound
Brean Hammond: *Gulliver's Travels*
Graham Holderness: *Hamlet*
Graham Holderness: *Women in Love*
Graham Holderness: *Wuthering Heights*
Jeannette King: *Jane Eyre*
Robyn Marsack: Sylvia Plath
Graham Martin: *Great Expectations*
Pam Morris: *Bleak House*
David B. Pirie: Shelley
Gareth Roberts: *The Faerie Queene*
Robert Shaughnessy: Three Socialist Plays
Jeremy Tambling: Narrative and Ideology
Jeremy Tambling: What is Literary Language?
Ronald Tamplin: Rhythm and Rhyme
Ronald Tamplin: Seamus Heaney
John Turner: *Macbeth*
Dennis Walder: Ted Hughes
John Ward: Thomas Hardy's Poetry
Roderick Watson: MacDiarmid
Ruth Whittaker: *Tristram Shandy*

RONALD TAMPLIN

Rhythm and Rhyme

Open University Press
Buckingham · Philadelphia

Open University Press
Celtic Court
22 Ballmoor
Buckingham
MK18 1XW

and
1900 Frost Road, Suite 101
Bristol, PA 19007, USA

First Published 1993

A catalogue record of this book is available from the British Library

Library of Congress Cataloging-in-Publication Data

Tamplin, Ronald.
    Rhythm and rhyme / Ronald Tamplin.
        p.   cm. — (Open guides to literature)
    Includes bibliographical references (p.   ) and index.
    ISBN 0-335-09452-X (hb)   ISBN 0-335-09451-1 (pb)
        1. English language—Rhythm. 2. English language—Versification.
    I. Title. II. Series.
PE1505.T35   1992
421'.6—dc20
                                                        92-10506
                                                        CIP

Typeset by Best-set Typesetter Limited, Hong Kong
Printed in Great Britain by J.W. Arrowsmith Limited, Bristol

To Charles Causley

Contents

Series Editor's Preface

The intention of this series is to provide short introductory books about major writers, texts, and literary concepts for students of courses in Higher Education which substantially or wholly involve the study of Literature.

The series adopts a pedagogic approach and style similar to that of Open University Material for Literature courses. *Open Guides* aim to inculcate the reading 'skills' which many introductory books in the field tend, mistakenly, to assume that the reader already possesses. They are, in this sense, 'teacherly' texts, planned and written in a manner which will develop in the reader the confidence to undertake further independent study of the topic. They are 'open' in two senses. First, they offer a three-way tutorial exchange between the writer of the *Guide*, the text or texts in question, and the reader. They invite readers to join in an exploratory discussion of texts, concentrating on their key aspects and on the main problems which readers, coming to the texts for the first time, are likely to encounter. The flow of a *Guide* 'discourse' is established by putting questions for the reader to follow up in a tentative and searching spirit, guided by the writer's comments, but not dominated by an over-arching and single-mindedly-pursued argument or evaluation, which itself requires to be 'read'.

Guides are also 'open' in a second sense. They assume that literary texts are 'plural', that there is no end to interpretation, and that it is for the reader to undertake the pleasurable task of discovering meaning and value in such texts. *Guides* seek to provide, in compact form, such relevant biographical, historical and cultural information as bears upon the reading of the text, and they point the reader to a selection of the best available critical discussions of it. They are not in themselves concerned to propose, or to counter, particular readings of the texts, but rather to put *Guide* readers in a position to do that for themselves. Experienced travellers learn to dispense with guides, and so it should be for readers of this series.

                                                              Graham Martin

Acknowledgements

I would like to thank various colleagues at the University of Exeter and Université Rennes 2 Haute Bretagne for conversations and particular helps assisting the writing of this book: Peter Corbin, Nicholas Eastwood, Myrddin Jones, Liliane Kerjan, Richard Maltby, Michael Packenham, Charles Page, André Rannou, Daniel Roulland, Martin Sorrell, Frances Williams and Peter Wiseman; Leslie Marchand and all the staff of UFR Anglais at Rennes 2 for their friendship and hospitality, under the benign impacts of which this book was mostly written; my students there, who genially listened to me working out bits of it in their courses, and two in particular, Véronique Jan and Rozanne Quere, whose expositions of Charles Causley's 'I am the Great Sun' helped me considerably; Charles Causley himself, to whom this book is dedicated as a small return for many years; Graham Martin, whose shrewd yet sympathetic editorial hand and patient heart exceeded anything I could reasonably expect; and my wife Anne, and Mary, Peter and Clare, whose great help was never just in the hope that I would get the thing finished.

Author and publisher are grateful for the following permissions to reprint copyright material: Faber and Faber and Alfred A. Knopf Inc. for an extract from *The Collected Works of Wallace Stevens*; for an extract from *William Carlos Williams. Collected Poems, 1909–1939. Vol. I.* Copyright 1938 by New Directions Pub. Corp. Reprinted by permission of New Directions; the author, Macmillan London Ltd and David Higham Associates Ltd for an extract from Charles Causley, *Collected Poems 1951–1975*.

1. Analysing Rhythm and Rhyme

I had better start with a confession. I have always found questions of rhythm and rhyme very difficult to teach. Rhythm is obviously present in poetry and is, equally obviously, very important. A regular rhythm is often precisely the way we first recognize a piece of writing as poetry. And 'if it doesn't rhyme and go tum-ti-tum, it isn't poetry' is still a basic notion for a lot of people, many of whom actively like poetry. If we are excited as we read poetry, rhythm is part of our excitement. But as soon as we start talking about iambics and anapaests and caesuras the whole thing seems incredibly dull – the very reverse of our delight in the thing we are trying, by these means, to describe. The most mechanical and least enthralling part of many student essays is the bit of metrical analysis and the account of a rhyme pattern, the two tacked on as a makeweight to an otherwise perceptive discussion of what the poem seems to be about.

One trouble is that, apart from its more obvious uses (for example, 'The poet reinforces the description of the train with rhythms like trainwheels drumming on the rails'), it is very difficult to assign 'meaning' to rhythm. The same is true of rhyme. 'Rhyme is used to comic effect' may sometimes be true, but it seldom gets us much further in our understanding of the poem. This difficulty in relating rhythm and rhyme to 'meaning' seems often to make our descriptions of them simply technical descriptions. And, of course, in some ways, they have to be. Arguably, it is necessary for analysts to construct definitions like 'a stress maximum is constituted by a syllable bearing linguistically determined stress that is greater than that of the two syllables adjacent to it in the same verse'[1] or 'the poetic function projects the principle of equivalence from the axis of selection into the axis of combination.'[2] It is necessary because, in a sense, analyses like these are providing a kind of overall algebra to describe the individual performances of the poets. But the kind of scientific exactness that seems to be on offer may, in fact, be illusory. Even the most intellectual of poets seldom talk about what they are doing in such ways.

In this book I will be proposing simplicity of expression and description rather than an illusory precision. The sheer difficulty of much linguistic analysis of the techniques of poetry actually makes the whole thing more difficult and certainly more forbidding than it really is. Equally, I will suggest ways by which we can talk about the 'meaning' of rhythm and rhyme rather than simply tabulate their presence. If poetic techniques can be shown to have meaning then we have solid reason for trying to see how they work, especially if it is through such an investigation that we are enabled to locate the meaning. We will not, then, be embarked on a journey through a maze of obscuring knowledge. So, two injunctions are at work in this account of rhythm and rhyme: first, keep it simple; second, look for a meaning behind the techniques.

It's time to look at a few lines of verse:

> All things that love the sun are out of doors;
> The sky rejoices in the morning's birth;
> The grass is bright with rain-drops; – on the moors
> The hare is running races in her mirth;
> And with her feet she from the plashy earth
> Raises a mist; that, glittering in the sun,
> Runs with her all the way, wherever she doth run.[3]

First, some hints as to how to go about looking at this from the point of view of its rhythms and rhymes. It's a good idea to write out the verse on a piece of paper, double-spacing the lines so that you have room to work. Next, read the lines aloud, slightly exaggerating any rhythm that your reading seems to suggest. This is an idea of Desmond Graham's, and it's a good one:[4] it helps to emphasize the natural musicality and variation in pitch in English verse.

Next, decide on a way to indicate the differing degrees of stress that the voice places on each syllable as it occurs in the sequence of the verse. The important thing is to distinguish as clearly as you can between a heavy stress and a light one. The two most usual descriptive systems are ˣ to indicate light stress and ˋ to

indicate heavy stress, or ˘ to indicate light stress and ¯ to indicate
heavy stress. These notations are placed above the syllables to
which they refer. Of the two I prefer the first pairing (thĕ cát) and
will use it throughout this book. It has two virtues. First, as a
visual metaphor; it seems visually to represent the differential
weight of light and heavy stress which is often a 'vertical' difference in pitch between low and high. For this the horizontal
marks ˘ and ¯ seem less expressive. Second, ˘ and ¯ have historically been used to indicate metrical values in classical Greek and
Latin verse. Greek and Latin metres were based on quantity (the
length of the sound of each syllable: ˘ as short and ¯ as long). I
think it's best not to use the same system in the English tradition
where stress usually matters more than quantity. But some books
do use it.

For rhyme, the usual system is to nominate the first rhyme-
sound and all subsequent words rhyming on the same sound as A,
the second rhyme-sound and all subsequent words rhyming on
that sound as B, the third as C and so on. In a poem that uses a
repeating stanza pattern you can use ABCD and so on for all
stanzas, even though different rhyme-sounds are introduced in
each stanza.

Two final things. You should count the number of syllables in
each line and make a note of how many there are at the end of
each line. And indicate with a question mark any doubts you have
about stress-values or the number of syllables. For example, is
'glittering' in line 6 of our example pronounced as three or two
syllables?

Now, with these fairly straightforward procedures in your
mind, mark the stresses and count the syllables in the verse lines
on page 2. (The lines are from Wordsworth's 'Resolution and
Independence'.) We will look at the rhymes later.

DISCUSSION

My account of these lines would be something like this:

All things that love the sun are out of doors;   10
The sky rejoices in the morning's birth;   10
The grass is bright with rain-drops; – on the moors   10
The hare is running races in her mirth;   10
And with her feet she from the plashy earth   10
Raises a mist; that, glittering in the sun,   11 ?
Runs with her all the way, wherever she doth run.   12

What do we notice? First, there is a dominant pattern both in stress and syllable-count. There are seven lines. Five of them clearly have ten syllables each. If we resolve 'glittering' to 'glitt'ring', as we would normally pronounce it, six of the lines have ten syllables each. With such regularity we could hazard the guess that the syllabically unambiguous line 7 has got twelve syllables quite deliberately. If we have any doubts about this we can check other stanzas in 'Resolution and Independence' to see whether their final lines have twelve syllables as well.

Next, heavy and light syllables seem fairly regularly to alternate – light/heavy, light/heavy – with five such units to each line except line 7, which has six. There are some variations from this, notably 'ràin-dròps; – ŏn thĕ mòors', 'Rǎisĕs' and 'Rŭns wǐth'. Whenever Wordsworth uses 'in' (lines 2, 4 and 6), the stress is ambiguous. An exaggerated 'tum-ti-tum' reading will give it a heavy stress, but the rhythms of conversation will probably lighten it. There is a similar ambiguity in line 5 with 'she from'. Most of these variations or ambiguities are best seen as a reversal of the dominant pattern in the lines where, starting from the beginning of the line, a light stress precedes a heavy stress in each pair of stresses. For verse of such regularity, this seems the simplest way to describe what is happening. Such a recurring verse unit (in this case ˣ`) is called a 'foot'.

In English verse, feet are usually of two syllables, as in this case, or of three syllables. A foot is, in effect, the shortest recurring combination of light and heavy stresses in any given line. Analysis by feet can be objected to on the grounds that it implies segmenting the continuous rhythm of the verse line. But we talk quite happily, in other situations, of 'beads' or 'rungs' without destroying our sense of the necklace or the ladder.

There are only four, or perhaps five, types of feet we need remember. They all have Greek-derived names and were originally applied to quantitative metres – that is, metres based on the length of the syllables used ('rid' being short, 'reed' being long). However, the names have been used long enough to describe stressed metres as well, for no real confusion to arise as to what we mean when we use them. The four are:

the iamb: ˣ`   thĕ hàre
the trochee: `ˣ   ràisĕs
the anapaest: ˣˣ`   ŏn thĕ mòors
the dactyl: `ˣˣ   ràisĕs ă

The fifth is

the spondee: `` ` rain-drops

Now, these descriptions do raise a problem. You will notice in my examples that my trochee and my dactyl are derived from different ways of scanning, or breaking into feet, Wordsworth's line 6. Look, though, more especially, at the line

The grass is bright with rain-drops; – on the moors

Using the feet detailed above, can you see various ways of scanning it (that is, describing its metrical characteristics)?

DISCUSSION

The actual stresses are clear enough:

The grass is bright with rain-drops; – on the moors

though I can imagine that in a public reading I might be inclined to give 'on' a heavy stress as well – 'on the moors' as distinguished from 'in the valleys' or 'down the mines'. But this is very much a question of an individual voice or imagination playing it by ear. The point about this is that, in a public reading, the poet is something of an actor and displacing an emphasis is a way of startling an audience, forcing it to attention. Curiously enough, this particular treatment of 'on' displaces the normal conversational voice but reinforces the metrical drive of the verse. At the same time, it forces a moment of unusual energy in the line: three succeeding heavy stresses and, in the whole line, six heavy stresses where five is the norm. More to the point, it might be a way of interpreting – giving value to Wordsworth's pause indicated in the punctuation – the dash. The sequence then is 'on the moors / The hare is running races'. I would read it that way, but, as I say, this is playing it by ear. Another legitimate reading would see what I have done as mechanical, following the iambic drive, and would, instead, savour the quiet, meditative reading that the light stressing seems to induce: 'on the moors / The hare is running races'. The poet or the actor will not, indeed, necessarily know how the particular performance will turn out nor remember afterwards. It is decided in the poise, the tension of the moment. Performance gives the lie to the excessive precision of much analysis. Performance is variable because it is alive. Analysis has meaning when it, too, remains alive and so admits variation and ambiguity. The more variation it recognizes, the less precision it can pretend to. Paradoxically, it will be the more accurate for that.

In practice, nearly every English word is capable of bearing a heavy stress. The meaning of 'You're not going out tonight' changes entirely as you emphasize 'You're' or 'not' or '-night' most prominently in the sentence. And consider 'the' – most unconsidered of words – in 'I'm talking about the gràss, not à farce'; or 'is' in 'The sky ìs bright tonight, isn't it?'; or 'with' in 'I said, "with ìce"'; and so on. Stress is relative, contextual, variable and part of the genius of the language, of its economy and subtlety. Poets, and not alone poets but all of us, daily, play on such possibilities for our best effects, our most persuasive understandings. Metre (ti-tum-ti-tum), and, more particularly, its less straight neighbour, 'rhythm', is not metronomic but rather the record of a voice in movement. This is part of the excitement of rhythm in poetry. It is part of the economy of its language, offering varieties of meaning in the one ordering of words.

Nevertheless, there is a tendency in English for nouns and verbs to carry within their accentual make-up, a heavy stress and for words that attend them, like 'the' and 'a'/'an', 'she'/'he'/'it'/ 'we'/'you'/'they', to be lightly, or at least more lightly, stressed. Because of this, and the recurrence in normal English of forms like 'the hare', 'her feet', 'he jumps', there is quite a good case for saying that English is naturally an iambic language. Or, perhaps better, that English speech tends naturally towards forming iambic patterns. It is only quite a good case – by no means an absolute one. As an alternative tendency, notice how often there also occur phrases like 'òut òf dòors', 'ìn the mòrning', 'òn the mòors', 'ìn her mìrth', 'wìth her feet', 'àll the wày', which might easily be felt to be anapaestic ($^{xx'}$). Notice, too, how often in my original scanning of the passage these elements have been absorbed – not, I think, unreasonably – into the iambic pattern which I am proposing is dominant in the lines. So, by way of the exaggeration I have suggested as a way of determining the dominant rhythm, the readings have been 'àre òut òf dòors', 'ìn her mìrth', 'ànd wìth her feet', 'àll the wày'. What seems to be happening is that the language of the passage has a dominant iambic drive with a hint of anapaestic variation.

But at this point we have to remember that we are dealing with ten-syllable lines. Ten divides naturally into 5 × 2, less easily into combinations of 3, though (2 × 3) + (2 × 2) is a clear possibility. And that thought seems to guarantee, if we were in doubt, that our basic description must be that the lines are

ten-syllabled iambics with occasional variations. If we were to
divide the line we began the discussion with into its shortest feet
(recurring combinations of stresses), we would have

The grass | is bright | with rain- | drops; – on | the moors

and the line is regularly iambic (that is, corresponding to the
dominant pattern that Wordsworth has established), but with a
variant, a trochee, in the fourth foot. I like to think of a trochee
(ˊˣ) as a reversed iambic (ˣˋ), of an anapaest (ˣˣˋ) as an extended
or lighter iambic (ˣˋ), and of a dactyl (ˊˣˣ) as an extended or
lighter trochee (ˊˣ). That way, all these variations can be elegantly
or economically derived from one simple binary opposition
between the light and the heavy stress. And elegance and economy
are central poetic impulses.

A less elegant way of describing this line would be

The grass | is bright | with rain- | drops; – ⁽ˣ⁾ | on the moors

allowing Wordsworth's dash the metrical value of an added
syllable – not carrying a stress-value at all, but a time-value, like a
musical beat. The virtue of this is that it more accurately describes
what happens in the line. Even more accurate would be to avoid
any notion of separating 'rain-' from 'drops'. Try speaking the
word and you will find that the two heavy stresses are not
separated but form one, albeit hyphenated, word. It's not going to
help much to call it a spondee (ˋ ˋ), or to see the unit 'drops; – on
the moors' as a choriambus (trochee + iamb). It's not going to
help because it's all too messy – and mildly ridiculous, too, in
terms of the normal habits of English verse writing. But equally
it's not the time to lose nerve and, like grammarians of the 1960s,
throw over simple description (such as we began with) in favour
of more and more complexity merely because the simple description does not provide a total description. A total description is less
important than an awareness of the basic drive of the verse.

My account, then, of the line

The grass is bright with rain-drops; – on the moors

would be that it is a variation upon a regular iambic line, its
second half involving ambiguous stress, a tendency towards
anapaestic pattern and a heavy pause which is capable of being
given metrical value. If I was pushed to it, I would say that. It
sounds like a diagnosis. But if I was reading it, I would play it by
ear and know that the little tunes that Wordsworth was playing

across the basic iambic drive were what rhythm in poetry is all about.

After that rather long account, teasing out a train of thought that, in fact, with practice occurs almost instantaneously and unnoticed in the mind, let's do one last piece of metrical practice, this time on Wordsworth's opening words: 'All things'. **What degrees of stress would you put on those two words?**

DISCUSSION

The fact that this is the opening phrase in what is clearly an iambic pentameter (an iambic line of ten syllables) naturally suggests that this would quite reasonably be scanned as 'Ăll things'. But 'All' seems to me to invite a heavy stress and to give more to the verse if it gets it. It is an attention-getting word and an easy way for a poet to mention everything without actually mentioning anything. Using it is often, in fact, sharp practice. Giving it a heavy stress doesn't really disturb our sense of the iambic thrust of the verse. The first position in the line is often used to give a word an extra emphasis. Visually, the opening word in any line was capitalized in the traditional typesetting for poetry. It comes immediately after the slight pause we cannot avoid making at the end of the previous line – which is, in any case, augmented here because 'All' is the beginning of a new stanza. And the fact that the metre would not normally put a heavy stress here tends again to bestow on the word the attention it demands if we do stress it. So I would want to read the opening as 'Àll things' and only then enter upon the iambic pattern.

I have mentioned quantity and time on a couple of occasions, and I'd like now to say a little about them as elements in English poetry. To understand quantity fully requires more knowledge of Greek and Latin practice than is necessary for a working understanding of most English metres. But there are ways in which an awareness of quantity can be very helpful in assessing the way English poetry is actually written. So, while not wishing to embroil us too much in unnecessary complexity, something has to be said: first because of the prestige in which classical metres stood, especially and crucially in the sixteenth century and again, by way of revival, in the nineteenth century; and second because quantity (that is, the time we take to say individual syllables) is a vital element in the particular practice of all poets. I am making a firm distinction, then, between the imitation of classical metres in English poetry, which is an interesting and murky backwater, and poets exploiting the quantitative values of particular English words, which is a vital part of all their practice. First, the metres.

Greek and Latin metres were governed by quantity. In analysis by quantity, all syllables were understood as long and or short and, in poetry, metrical value was assigned to them as they fitted into patterns understood as combinations of long and/or short syllables. In English poetry, by contrast, metrical value is habitually determined by stress, the degree of stress on any given syllable having no necessary connection with the length of that syllable. Thus a Latin *iambus* is a combination of short followed by long (˘ ¯); an English iamb is a combination of light stress followed by heavy stress (ˣ ˋ). 'The cat' is, in its most frequent stressing, an English iamb, but according to its quantitative values it would, were it to appear in a classical metre, be not an *iambus* but a *trochaeus* (English, trochee), ¯ ˘. In English 'the cat' and 'an owl' are, again most frequently, metrical equivalents – both iambs. In quantitative terms their values are the reverse of each other: 'the cat' is ¯ ˘ and 'an owl' is ˘ ¯. In a single foot this will not make much difference in a verse line, but, if you construct whole lines in English based on the classical quantitative rules as they might be supposed to operate when applied to English, then the result is very distinctive and a bit untoward.

Consider this example from Spenser, who took part in Elizabethan attempts to match classical metres to the English language:

Sēe yēe thĕ | blīndefŏuld | ēd prĕtĭe | Gŏd thāt | fēathĕrĕd | Ārchĕr
Ōf Lŏu | ers Mĭsĕr | ĭes | whĭch mākĕth | hĭs blŏudĭe | Gāme?[5]

The quantitative scansion here is offered by Enid Hamer in her book *The Metres of English Poetry* (1930), but, whether she's right or wrong in her account of the lines, it's not altogether clear what Spenser had in mind in terms of English syllabic quantity. One thing he hasn't done, though, is to render classical metrical length by English stress: it is a genuine attempt to write classically modelled quantitative verse. To say it sounds outlandish is perhaps only to say it didn't catch on. But it may be that the wrench of writing English verse without a primary regard to stress is too much for the language.

This suggestion has more cogency if we look at the same poet's '*Iambicum Trimetrum*', attempting a classical iambic metre. Here a binary rhythm more assimilable to the grain of English is showing through, and we could scan the lines, using stress, as something like English iambics:

Unhappie verse, the witnesse of my unhappie state
Make thy selfe flutt'ring wings of thy fast flying thought,
And fly forth unto my Love, wheresoever she be.[6]

Again, we have no clear knowledge of how Spenser himself would
have wanted to scan these lines, because we cannot be sure how
and with what degree of freedom he would have applied the
classical rules to English. But since our stress-based scansion is
clearly possible, it suggests that he might have arrived at such lines
more naturally and with less labour by following an English stress
pattern rather than rules adopted from classical practice. And this,
at the level of metric, was to be the more usual way for English
poets to shape their lines – by stress, not quantity. However, this
is not to say that some interesting verse has not been arrived at
through the use of quantitative metres. The Victorian Arthur
Hugh Clough, for example, wrote 'Amours de Voyage' (1858)
in classical hexameters. The poem is written as an exchange of
letters:

> Dear Eustatio, I write that you may write me an answer,
> Or at least to put us again *en rapport* with each other.
> Rome disappoints me much, – St. Peter's, perhaps, in especial;
> Only the Arch of Titus and view from the Lateran please me:
> This, however, perhaps, is the weather, which truly is horrid.[7]

The unusual relaxed formality of this is due very much to the
choice of an unmistakably poetic rhythm, yet one that has few
associations in traditional English verse and so raises no expectations as to what the subject should be and how it ought to be
handled. It doesn't sound 'like poetry ought to sound' and so is
oddly modern. But it has order – a mark of art.

More important to the habits of English poetry, though, is the
use of quantity to create special effects and, if you like, verbal
music. The length of sounds ('rid' short, 'reed' long) is always at
work, slowing or speeding the words we hear and so what we
understand by them. Diphthongs in English ('raid') are generally
held to be long, combining, as they do, more than one vowel
sound.

**Can you see how the length of the sounds moulds our percep-
tions in these two passages from Robert Browning's poem 'The
Bishop Orders his Tomb at St. Praxed's Church'?**

> Life, how and what is it? As here I lie
> In this state-chamber, dying by degrees,
> Hours and long hours in the dead night, I ask
> 'Do I live, am I dead?' Peace, peace seems all.

and

All *lapis*, all, sons! Else I give the Pope
My villas! will ye ever eat my heart?
Ever your eyes were as a lizard's quick,
They glitter like your mother's for my soul.[8]

DISCUSSION

In the first passage, all the lines end with long syllables, three of
them with sequences of three, and one of them with four: 'here I
lie', 'night, I ask', 'Peace, peace seems all.' The second line also
contains a sequence of four longs: 'state-chamber, dy-'. These
sequences contrast with the peremptory end of the opening question, 'Life, how and what is it?' It is not unreasonable to say that,
in the context, these sequences of longs encourage our perception
of life extending, first through the process of dying and then into
eternity (peace) – all this in response to the arrest of 'and what is
it?' I stress that we can only relate such meanings to a context: the
one that the meaning of the words is primarily supplying. Browning reinforces the meaning he is after by the way he places and
chooses his quantities.

There is a second problem about applying quantity to English
poetry, and that is the sheer difficulty of doing it. Most English
words can be treated rather elastically in terms of quantity. For
example, 'long' in 'Hours and long hours' will, in performance,
almost certainly, be dwelt on, lengthened: just as a singer can
take more than one note to render a single syllable. 'Night', in
'the dead night' will almost certainly be read staccato – another
peremptory arrest, in fact. It seems to me that 'flying by the trees',
for example, is 'shorter' than 'dying by degrees'. And I find it hard
to think that 'I hate Moorgate' is, in fact, longer than 'Jim loves
West Ham'. Try it. Such differences can be measured in micro-
seconds in a laboratory but I think that, without that special aid,
what we recognize are in most cases psychological rather than
physiological differences.

In the second passage, something slightly different is operating. There are a number of short *i*s – '*lapis*', 'give', 'villas', 'will',
'lizard's', 'quick', 'glitter'. Now, there's nothing special that we
associate with short *i*s – they don't signal greed or anything like
that. But, in the structure of the passage, I suggest they anticipate
and reinforce the end of the sequence they are part of, and this
image, of the glittering eyes, does, in fact, signal greed. Be careful

of this, though. It is the image, the association we have with the unnaturally alert eyes, not missing a trick, that gives rise to the meaning, not any inevitable effect of the sound. Once the association is made, though, we see, as with a building, other features, in this case, the preceding short *is*, anticipating and echoing the most important feature. This is primarily an effect of quantity.

More often than not, variation in quantity is used simply to introduce variety, texture, into the writing, to pace the lines. Consider for yourself, as an exercise – if it has to be! – the first eight lines of this sonnet by John Donne. What are the effects of Donne's variations in quantity? Does his choice of words influence the pace at which you read it aloud? I'll put my ideas down at the end of the book, in note 9 to chapter 1.

> At the round earth's imagin'd corners, blow
> Your trumpets, Angels, and arise, arise
> From death, you numberless infinities
> Of souls, and to your scatter'd bodies go,
> All whom the flood did, and fire shall o'erthrow,
> All whom war, dearth, age, agues, tyrannies,
> Despair, law, chance, hath slain, and you whose eyes,
> Shall behold God, and never taste death's woe.[9]

To return to the passage from Wordsworth we started from, could you now tabulate the rhyme-scheme Wordsworth is using? You'll find the system I suggested on page 3. Can you see that the rhymes – and rhymes in general – serve any particular purpose in the texture of the verse?

DISCUSSION

Rhyme has a very important function in poetry. It is a device which emphasizes the interrelationship of the various elements of a poem and it is a structural echo of those other relationships – prime among them, of course, metaphor. A poem is, in a strong sense, a demonstration of the possibilities of relationship; and all its elements, however unconscious we are of them and however concealed, even subliminal, they are, conspire to that demonstration. A rhyme-scheme is one of the most important of these 'netting' effects. In the case of 'Resolution and Independence', the rhyme-scheme is ABABBCC. The first four lines are interlocked and then slide smoothly into couplets. From a poet's point of view, it is rather a satisfying, well-made stanza, balanced but, by the introduction of the new third rhyme (C), seeming to lead on to something new. I say 'from a poet's point of view'. Many poets are reassured by perceptible shape and structure, however various the means they use to arrive at it. They know that, whatever else, they have 'made' something. Rhyme, its chiming recurrence, is one of the strongest shape-giving devices.

This is all very well, but I'm making it sound a bit private. How does the reader enter into that charmed circle? Easily enough, I think. Notice how the rhymes confirm a shape for the statement Wordsworth is making. The confirmation acts both on the eye, as we see the words 'doors', 'birth', 'moors', 'mirth' and so on, and also for the ear, as we speak the verse. At the same time, part of the skill of rhyming is that, if the poet wants them to, rhymes, certainly in lines of ten syllables and longer, can be made to efface themselves, not exactly hiding but not obtruding either. Wordsworth helps maintain this balance between recognition and surprise by not end-stopping the rhymes 'moors' and 'earth' but letting them run syntactically into their following lines. End-stopping – that is, punctuating the lines so that strong syntactic pauses occur at the ends of the lines – is, of course, one way of drawing attention to the rhymes and so to the poetic shape. Once we start to take pleasure from the existence of such shape, we begin to inhabit the mental world of the poet. Once we see that such shape is itself a metaphor for all the relationships in sound and meaning that the poem proposes, we are deep within that world.

One further point. See how Wordsworth produces, without any sense of jingle, a little internal rhyme – 'sun', 'Runs', 'run' – and notice, too, the balance of that final line that seems to crown the stanza. The line divides into four three-syllabled units, three of them with the same rhythm, all enclosed between the rhyme at the beginning and the end of the line. You could set the line up as a little poem:

> Runs with her
> All the way,
> Wherever
> She doth run.

If you do that, the internal music of the line becomes very clear: the rhyme-sounds 'Runs'/'run' and 'her'/'Wherever'; the alliteration 'with', 'way', 'Wherever'; the verbal echoes 'with' and 'doth'. I do not suggest that these effects are heavily deliberated by Wordsworth. Rather, that the mind of a poet, as it is normally working, thinks in terms of sonic and rhythmic design. In a sense all these effects are 'rhymes' – a sounding together. Rhyme, properly so-called, is only a more emphatic type of the poet's basic mental procedure, to set the materials of a poem in relationship.

One last thing for you to comment on. The line, if it divides naturally into 4 × 3, has twelve syllables. We had already noticed this when we did our syllable-count. Before you work out what effect this lengthening of the line from ten to twelve syllables has on the end of the stanza, look at a more elaborate use of varying line-length. Here is Thomas Hardy's 'During Wind and Rain'.

> They sing their dearest songs –
> He, she, all of them – yea,
> Treble and tenor and bass,
>   And one to play;
> With the candles mooning each face . . .
>   Ah, no; the years O!
> How the sick leaves reel down in throngs!
>
> They clear the creeping moss –
> Elders and juniors – aye,
> Making the pathways neat
>   And the gardens gay;
> And they build a shady seat . . .
>   Ah, no; the years, the years;
> See, the white storm-birds wing across!
>
> They are blithely breakfasting all –
> Men and maidens – yea,
> Under the summer tree,
>   With a glimpse of the bay,
> While pet fowl come to the knee . . .
>   Ah, no; the years O!
> And the rotten rose is ript from the wall.
>
> They change to a high new house,
> He, she, all of them – aye,
> Clocks and carpets and chairs
>   On the lawn all day,
> And brightest things that are theirs . . .
>   Ah, no; the years, the years;
> Down their carved names the rain-drop ploughs.[10]

Do a syllable-count and then see whether the numbers you come up with will allow you to talk about a consistent pattern.

DISCUSSION

I arrive at these numbers.

Stanza 1:   6 6 7 4 8 5 8
Stanza 2:   6 6 6 5 7 6 8
Stanza 3:   8 5 6 6 7 5 10
Stanza 4:   7 6 6 5 7 6 8

As far as syllables go, there's no attempt to maintain a constant count for equivalent lines through the four stanzas. You can tell this was not the poet's intention not just because a constant syllable-pattern is not there but because it would have been so easy to put it there if Hardy had wanted to. Stanzas 2 and 4 are almost the same anyway so they would seem to indicate the syllable-pattern that we could speak of as lurking within the poem. You could regularize the whole poem to 6 6 6 5 7 6 8 like this:

They sing their dearest songs –
He, she, all of them – yea,
Treble, tenor and bass,
And one more to play;
The candles mooning each face . . .
Ah, no; the years O!
How the sick leaves reel down in throngs!

They clear the creeping moss –
Elders and juniors – aye,
Making the pathways neat
And the garden gay;
And they build a shady seat . . .
Ah, no; the years, the years;
See, the white storm-birds wing across!

They blithely breakfast all –
Men and maidens – yea,
Under the summer tree,
With a glimpse of bay,
While pet fowl come to the knee . . .
Ah, no; the years O!
The rotten rose rips from the wall.

They take a high new house,
He, she, all of them – aye,
Clocks and carpets and chairs
On the lawn all day,
And brightest things that are theirs . . .
Ah, no; the years, the years;
Down their carved names the rain-drop ploughs.

So, if it's as easy as that and the poem is more or less intact, Hardy clearly isn't worried about exact syllable-counts. But equally, if the syllable-count pattern is as close to an exact count as this version shows it is, then Hardy is clearly sensitive to a recurring pattern of varying line-lengths. It's consistent through all the stanzas. In his pattern, no line is ever shorter than the fourth and/or the sixth line, and no line is longer than the seventh line, the last line of each stanza. Hardy represents this consistent pattern of variable lines visually, by indenting the lines in a regular pattern. In my version I didn't do this in order to show by contrast how carefully Hardy's line-pattern has, in fact, been established. **Now, what is the effect of all this variation, do you think?**

DISCUSSION

To begin with the visual pattern. This immediately establishes variation in the line and continuity in the stanzaic form. This is true of all variable-line stanzas, but in this case the poem is itself about change and continuity – the passage of time, its constant ravages and our haunted backward looks – so Hardy uses his form to reinforce his theme. The stanza shape is particularly songlike, and this association too adds a sense of poignancy to the movement of the poem. It is like a Victorian drawing-room ballad, made savage by a singer who sees too much, too deep into the heart of things. Hardy's form, then, works like a kind of visual refrain. But he has a verbal refrain too – the lines which mention 'the years'. Here again he emphasizes change as well as continuity, by the simple but very clever device of varying those lines in a consistent pattern through the stanzas, so that stanza 1 matches stanza 3 and stanza 2 matches stanza 4. And along with that there is a refrain-like balance in the events of each stanza. To see how aware Hardy is of the way his structures can echo his theme – *be* that theme – look at the immaculately consistent punctuation, the dashes and the fading dots and even the regular placings of commas and semicolons.

I would like to take this question of form one step further. Line-length, to a large degree, governs the unit of space that thoughts characteristically occupy in a poem. It is not going too far to say that a line is, more often than not, a 'thinking-space'. As you vary the lengths of the thinking-spaces, so you regulate the way the thoughts come. In this poem they do not come regular as clockwork but broken, differentiated. Hardy is not like a tiger in a cage, marking out the day in an endless pacing of its length. Instead he stops short, goes a little further, a little further, stops halfway, goes on. Instead of rules he has constants. However he varies it, mutters and inches forward, he *will* arrive, the course of gloomy foreboding held up but never arrested. Indeed it reaches beyond the end of the poem: as long as there is weather and time, the carved names will be ploughed by the rain, the rose ripped by the wind. For the metronome of regular beat, Hardy has substituted the inevitability that, however the lines fall, the end must be the same. He writes not by metronome but by the remorseless music of time, which may seem to be stayed but never can be.

Of course a variable line-length can produce other musics. Eventually any music is governed by the voice of the poet and the occasion of the poem. In this case it is Hardy's voice that draws out one line, long beyond all the others, to plant in it the word 'rotten', with its savage sense of decay and spoil, the corruption of the world's condition. It was this line that my syllabically exact version of the poem could not contain: I managed the 'rotten' but I lost the force of the intransitive verb, the stricken powerlessness of the diseased rose.

And the rotten rose is ript from the wall.

For the regular, Hardy invites us to contemplate the inevitable.

All this is to look at line-length as an aspect of metrical variation. It is just this possibility of variation that Wordsworth is working with when he uses a twelve-syllable line to close his stanza in 'Resolution and Independence'. The twelve-syllable line, by the way, is called an alexandrine.[11] Hardy too has, in every case, made the last line of his stanzas in 'During Wind and Rain' longer than his average line, by between two and four syllables. An addition of as little as two syllables at the end of the stanza will give a poet just a little more room to move, to close the stanza's pattern and expand the dominant thought. In Wordsworth's case it was to build a line with a little pattern of four three-syllable units and a consequent sense of resolution. In Hardy's case it is to allow in each stanza a packed climactic flourish, the final words confirming the drive of the thought in the whole sequence.

I have wanted to make one major point in examining the use of variable line-lengths. But there are other questions you could ask yourself about Hardy's methods here. I talked about refrains. Can you see uses of refrain in the poem that haven't been mentioned? Is one of the effects of refrain to throw another net of rhyme over not just the stanza but the whole poem? What is the effect of that? And are there any other types of sound-associations in the poem, on the model of what we were able to see in the final line of the extract from Wordsworth? Would it, for example, be only fanciful to suggest that the alliteration in Hardy's fourth stanza helps to confirm the sense in the poem of an insistent order, established not so much by rules but by inevitable tendency?

So where have we got to in this chapter? Well we've looked at some examples of poets at work, concentrating not so much on what their words mean as on the structures they use. Clearly there is no way these two things can be entirely separated, even for the purposes of analysis – each is too deeply implicated in the other. We have been looking particularly at stress, quantity, rhyme and associated uses of sound, syllables and line-length. These are the materials of poetry, and we will be returning to them throughout this book, which is very much a workbook. We have also put together some basic terms and procedures to help our analyses. At the same time, though I have not talked much about the 'meaning' of rhythm, there has been a hint in what we have observed that we are not dealing simply with devices. Rather it is that, properly understood, all these devices will propel us into talk of meaning. The next chapter will be an attempt at that.

To conclude then – since this is a workbook – to add to the exercises I've suggested along the way, here is an early poem – a five-finger exercise – of my own, its principal elements, technically regarded, being hidden rhymes and a mixture of line length or, put another way, syllable count. I say 'five-finger exercise' deliberately. When I wrote the poem, as a beginning poet, I was trying a number of things in the way of training myself. I was particularly anxious not to use iambic rhythms, and I adopted strategies to avoid them. I was also very concerned not to use adjectives, unless they were really working, and to use rhyme and connective, reverberative structures but not to use them in the usual ways. I wanted to hide them but to retain their unconscious effect. Of course it was conscious to me, so there was that enjoyment of the 'made' construct that I spoke of earlier. I have called this an 'exercise', but obviously, if I was that concerned about it, I wanted to write a poem that meant something and there is a particular structure of meaning too. I say that for the sake of complete-ness, but I want you to concentrate on the techniques. There is a decided structure, both of line-length and, in the first and last couplets, rhyme. The effect of the rhymes is to construct an enclosing device around the whole poem. Can you see the structures of rhyme and syllable I was using? If you can, then you have certainly absorbed what we have been working out in this chapter. Incidentally, I have said nothing about stress in relation to the poem. Again, this is deliberate. Perhaps you noticed I didn't say anything about stress with the Hardy poem either. If you respect the basic pulse of your verse, stress will often look after itself. Anyway I'll leave you with the poem, and in note 12 to chapter 1, at the end of the book, I'll tell you what I thought I was doing when I wrote it, insofar as I can after the long wearing away of time. But you work it out first, with the clues I've given.

Considerations of a Courier Visitation

Avoid shadows, forest. Most, avoid men.
Do not ask the way, find it. Stick to it.

   Advice. Shoes must be thin, thick,
   Soft shoes, no shoes. Advice against
   Advice, circumstance against
   Advice. Just tell me where the shoes are,
   Or the only decent oil.
   Outside, this hail of voices: within
   Me, secretly rehearsing,
   The dispatch waiting for the right
   Ears. The general will smile
   And call attendance on the courier.

Then, as they laugh, I listen. The long void
Is past, their welcome in my message too.[12]

2. The Meaning of Poetic Patterns

In this chapter I want to concentrate briefly on a less technical aspect of the methods of poetry: the question of whether they might, in themselves, have 'meaning' – a less technical question, certainly, but not less difficult. Again, I want to keep the terms of our discussion as straightforward as I can.

I hope that in the last chapter you didn't, at any point, feel compelled to say, 'Well, OK, but what has all this got to do with poetry?' or feel that your pleasure in the poetry had been stopped dead in its tracks by over-discussion and by talking about the wrong things. First, you should make sure the poetry *is* still there.

If you look back at the Wordsworth or the Hardy and read it aloud, it may even be that it is more fully there. The way to deal with any analysis, over-elaborate or not, is to let it sink into your mind as background only and to read the poem again, with full pleasure. This, I hope you will see, is not the same as reading it without, in the first place, putting all that thought in.

All the same, the very frequent sense that the study of technique is stultifying rather than enlightening does seem to be a barrier for a lot of people. It goes along with a feeling that it makes poetry an 'artificial' rather than a 'natural' form of expression. **Would you want to say, first, that poetry is 'artificial' and, second, that it is especially the attention that poets (and teachers) lavish or once lavished on patterns of rhythm and rhyme that makes it 'artificial'?**

DISCUSSION

These are fundamental questions and need to be put as bluntly as they have been here. They go to the heart of what poetry is doing, and so we need briefly to give at least a temporary response to them early in our discussion. Insofar as they are also very complicated questions and wide-ranging in their implications, we will have to examine our responses and take them deeper at a later stage. Here I want to propose a response along the following lines. First, for art to be artificial is, in fact, natural. Novels, symphonies, popular songs, football, chess and so on – most of the things people enjoy – are characterized by structures that are artificial rather than simply 'given'. They need laws to function by, structures to keep them from disintegrating, techniques of preparation to render them 'cooked' and not 'raw'.[1] But, second, I wish to go further and suggest that it is precisely in this pursuit of and delight in structure that they are most lifelike: that the world in its natural state, as much as the manmade world, is subject to its own firmly laid structures of chemical interaction, ecological chain, alternation and rhythm. And so when art is structured, successive, rhythmic in its pulse, it is modelled on the deep structure of the world and not simply responding to a set of manmade, arbitrary rules. If this seems to 'up the ante' rather precipitately – 'I only asked,' you may say – then let's initially, in this chapter, concentrate on whether structure governs at least the other arts, and not only poetry. **Do you think, for example, that it makes sense to talk about the rhythm of a painting or a piece of sculpture?**

DISCUSSION

Patrick Heron, one of the finest of English abstract painters, has written an essay which sets out as a discussion of the pottery of Bernard Leach, the most distinguished of England's twentieth-century potters. It is called 'Submerged Rhythm' and, really, its implications could sustain the rest of this book.[2] Heron begins by quoting Leach's description of the newly thrown pot, still wet: its

> volumes, open spaces and outlines are parts of a living whole; they are thoughts, controlled forces in counterpoise of rhythm. A single intuitive pressure on the spinning wet clay, and the whole pot comes to life; a false touch and the expression is lost.[3]

Two things are immediately striking here. Leach, while clearly able to distinguish, for the purpose of talking about them, between volumes, outlines, thoughts and clay, none the less perceives them as one, and made one as 'controlled forces in counterpoise of rhythm'. Second, there is for the potter an indivisible relationship between the pot, which we may view as an art object, though one with an undoubted function, and the process which brings it into being. This process is characterized by movement, both mechanically aided – the spinning potter's wheel – and physical – the pressure of fingers, thumb and hand upon the clay. The pot is a bodily expression, though one in which, as Leach himself said, 'every movement hangs like frozen music'.[4]

Later in his essay Heron turns to his own practice as a painter and generalizes from it. He writes:

> It is possible to argue that all painters are *primarily* concerned with the definition of space: it is possible to believe that all painters – whether they are representational or abstract ('non-figurative', as I prefer to say) are all more vitally concerned with giving concrete, tangible reality to certain abstract rhythms, certain patterns or formal configurations, than to specific, individual forms.[5]

He goes on to speak of the twentieth-century French painter Georges Braque creating or releasing 'a new rhythm'. Heron describes such a new rhythm as pervading a painting, 'dominating its forms, dictating its character and above all, determining its intervals'. He further says that such a rhythm cannot come about 'without drawing on the deepest and most unexpected resources of human feeling or consciousness'.[6]

Finally, as he returns to the discussion of pottery, Heron identifies in the work of Leach and some other twentieth-century potters a quality which he calls 'submerged rhythm'. He says of it:

We feel a powerful pulse in their pots: a rhythm that seems at its most emphatic just below the glazed surface. This is also a characteristic of natural forms – logs; boulders that have been washed by the sea; or even in the human figure, where the structural form is *below* the surface of the flesh – the bone is under the muscle.[7]

There is a new assertion here: that the natural world is also characterized by rhythmic structure. And in developing the idea, Heron again calls on Braque, who

has said that the painter should put himself in rhythmic or formal sympathy with nature: he should not imitate. By doing the first he gets close to that natural reality he loves: by the second, he estranges himself from nature.[8]

In terms of Braque's distinctions here, can you see how, at a deeper level than we began with, we might apply *both* the words 'natural' and 'artificial' to the rhythms of an art?

DISCUSSION

At the obvious level – which is always the place to start and often the best place to finish – we could say that, insofar as we accept that the natural world has a rhythm, when we place ourselves in 'sympathy' with it then we will also be natural and rhythmic at the same time. Of course we may not be too keen to accept that the natural world has rhythm and design – or, indeed, we may not have the degree of scientific knowledge which we would need in order to say yes or no. Perhaps we are imposing on the world, as a means of describing it, a rhythm which is not in fact there. But to see such a rhythm seems, at the least, a valuable metaphor for the structures that science has revealed and that are our commonly attested experience.

But it is the second element in Braque's account that I find more intriguing and suggestive in the present context: that by merely imitating the natural world we estrange ourselves from it. To express our 'rhythmic or formal sympathy' with the natural world, therefore, we must respond in our own terms, giving our shapes to celebrate the shapes we perceive as present to us but distinct from us. Our rhythms will be made by us, made by art – that is, artificial – but will have a life of their own, to echo the life that precedes them in the natural world. In that sense, then, they are also natural. Heron concludes his essay by speaking of 'man's will to form'. He writes, 'If I believe this sense of form is of immeasurable importance to mankind – that may well be because, for me, the moral and the aesthetic have a single identity. Ethics are the aesthetics of behaviour.'[9]

Now it may seem perverse to invoke the world of ethics and the expanses of the universe in a discussion that is supposed to be about things like whether it's useful to describe a line as an iambic pentameter or not. But I believe firmly that the difficulty we have in getting ourselves worked up about poetic structures arises precisely because, in a world of woe, one where there are plenty of pressing meanings to hand, poetic structures don't seem all that important. The difficulty is in giving them an adequate 'meaning'. And yet, to listen to Heron, Braque and Leach, it is not just that the rhythms of art have meaning but that it seems to be the meaning that they most fully acknowledge.

Even at this point we might say, yes, but these are all artists not poets. They perceive rhythm as meaning simply because they do not use words in their art. Rhythm and design are their only meanings. Words give poets more direct meanings. For poets, rhythms, rhymes and the rest are only means to elucidate those meanings. **In fact, might there not be something dubious about such large-scale analogies between the practice of one type of art – painting and pottery – and another – poetry?**

DISCUSSION

It is clearly true that different arts make us aware of different types of meaning. And the rationales behind the techniques used to put those meanings before us are not so simply interchangeable. The American poet Wallace Stevens balances the two sides well. He wrote:

> There is a universal poetry that is reflected in everything. This remark approaches the idea of Baudelaire that there exists an un-ascertained and fundamental aesthetic, or order, of which poetry and painting are manifestations, but of which, for that matter, sculpture or music or any other aesthetic realization would equally be a manifestation. Generalizations as expansive as these: that there is a universal poetry that is reflected in everything or that there may be a fundamental aesthetic of which poetry and painting are related but dissimilar manifestations, are speculative. One is better satisfied by particulars.[10]

One way of particularizing the parallel suggested here might be to apply to poetry Braque's idea that the artist must render the natural world in a non-imitative way. Now poetry renders the natural world certainly. Prime among the elements it renders is speech. But it renders speech in a heightened way, giving it an enhanced rhythm and features like rhyme and alliteration. The ideas that 'people don't talk poetry', that 'it's not poetry if it doesn't rhyme' and the folk reaction that, if by chance you stumble on a rhyme while you're talking, 'you're a poet and you don't know it' are all popular testimony to the strangeness of poetry. Poetry is a type of alternative speech, not an imitation of everyday speech. Rhyme and metrical pulse are key ways for making it different. So Braque's idea can be applied directly to the way poets work too. And of course, insofar as poets use the words everybody uses, make their syntax intelligible to speakers who are not necessarily poets and assume that what they write may be spoken, so their poems maintain a kinship with habitual social speech. But it is a blood relationship only, not a question of identical twins.

More imaginatively, let us examine how some poets have elaborated the same image that stimulated Heron's insights – the vase, pot or jar – to see how it contributes to a generalized aesthetic conclusion. Perhaps the most famous description of a pot in English poetry is John Keats's 'Ode on a Grecian Urn'. You will find the poem on page 29. This urn, which tells stories ('sylvan historian'), whose 'folk' play music ('pipes'), but a strange music 'of no tone' played to the 'spirit' and involved with love and sacrifice, death and desolation, peace and piety, time and eternity, is a supremely shaped and patterned object:

> O Attic shape! Fair attitude! with brede
> Of marble men and maidens overwrought.

A 'silent form', a phrase which expresses the urn's aesthetic function as a piece of pottery (remember Leach's 'frozen music') is paralleled by 'Cold Pastoral!' which places it in the literary and poetic tradition of pastoral verse. Keats has no particular problem about investing one art with the attributes of another. And indeed Heron, in his aphoristic conclusion, 'the moral and the aesthetic have a single identity. Ethics are the aesthetics of behaviour,' may well be echoing the assertion in the 'Ode on a Grecian Urn' that 'Beauty is truth, truth beauty'.

In the twentieth century, Wallace Stevens has also addressed the theme in his 'Anecdote of the Jar':

> I placed a jar in Tennessee,
> And round it was, upon a hill.
> It made the slovenly wilderness
> Surround that hill.
>
> The wilderness rose up to it,
> And sprawled around, no longer wild.

The jar was round upon the ground
And tall and of a port in air.

It took dominion everywhere.
The jar was gray and bare.
It did not give of bird or bush,
Like nothing else in Tennessee.[11]

Enigmatic as this poem is, it is certainly suggesting that art ('the jar') has the ability to give order to a random and disordered nature ('the slovenly wilderness'), and the idea that it is the only thing in Tennessee that 'did not give of bird or bush' seems to be saying something similar to Braque's idea that, while aesthetic form will stand in relationship to nature, it will none the less be distanced from it.

Lastly T. S. Eliot in 'Burnt Norton', the first of his *Four Quartets*, writes:

Words move, music moves
Only in time; but that which is only living
Can only die. Words, after speech, reach
Into the silence. Only by the form, the pattern,
Can words or music reach
The stillness, as a Chinese jar still
Moves perpetually in its stillness.[12]

We would have to say that Eliot, in this move from time to eternity by way of words, is not just concerned with questions of art. But it is the importance of pattern that is most relevant to us here. It enables words after we have exhausted their effect as speech – as human communication – to reach into a silent world beyond the world of time. And Eliot manages to convey that same balance between stillness and movement in the form of the jar that Keats also achieves by juxtaposing the narrative events in the painted stories on the urn with the stillness of the urn and the arrested nature of painting itself.

So much for analogies with painting and the visual arts. But music might provide an even more fruitful analogy. Both Keats and Eliot, interestingly, invoke music in the same contexts as they talk of the Grecian urn and the Chinese jar, and while they are considering large aesthetic questions. Keats's rhythms when he talks about music are themselves – can we say it? – musical. 'Heard melodies are sweet, but those unheard / Are sweeter' and so on. Eliot, in fact, couples the two arts: 'Words move, music moves ... Only by ... the pattern, / Can words or music ...'

I asked whether we could use the word 'musical' to describe a particular rhythm in Keats. By implication we should consider whether it is used appropriately to describe many effects of poetry. Where music and poetry are concerned, are we talking about 'sister' arts rather than just cousins? Would, then, the type of rhythmic and formal parallels that we have been able to adduce with painting be even more persuasive when we compare music with poetry – evidence from the one giving us direct access to the condition of the other?

DISCUSSION

Well, I have to answer 'yes and no'. First, we don't have to argue about the presence of rhythm in music. It's there for all to hear and tap their feet to. And the same goes for all the aspects of sound – pitch, stress, beat, time and so on. We can use these terms interchangeably in describing both music and poetry. Both music and poetry are structures built from sound, after all. And where there are not exact equivalences, there are clear parallels – bars and feet, rhymes and repeating phrases. A term like 'counterpoint' is frequently borrowed from music to describe the rhythmic complexity of a verse line where the poet has created an interplay between a basic metrical beat and a variation on it and where we are able to feel two rhythms simultaneously at work. When I was writing about Wordsworth's 'little tunes' on page 7 I could have used the term 'counterpoint' (Latin, *'punctus contra punctum'*: 'note against note').

It would open up too many questions to go into the origins of poetic speech and song, but the weight of speculation, and to some degree of the evidence, suggests an intimacy between them: that rhythmic actions and our earliest acts of praise and propitiation involved rhythmic and melodic vocalization, that is, music and words together. If we wish to see it so, the voice, projected through the cavity of the mouth, its sounds varied by movements of the facial muscles and the tongue, by the shaping of the lips, is a wind instrument. A column of air is being subjected to stops and induced vibrations. So speech as much as song is musical. Voices in ordinary speech have differential pitch (highness or lowness of sound) and differential timbre (tonal quality) depending on various physical factors – our sex, our cranial cavities and so on – just as they do in song, or just as different musical instruments do – violins and cellos, or flutes and oboes, for example.

In myth, too, the same intimacy is preserved. Poetry is spoken of as 'song' and the poet as a 'singer', especially where a cosmic order, the tuning of the spheres, is concerned. Thus poetic speech, through its intimacy with song, is 'estranged' from everyday usage but not divorced from it. Poets, I suppose would have argued, and some still would, that in such mythic reaches speech attains its full potential. Thinking of this sort is at work in Eliot's 'Words, after speech, reach / Into the silence' and it's why, in the Bible, the angels sing at the birth of Jesus (Luke 2:13–14), they don't just make an announcement.

What techniques the angels used when they sang must remain speculation – if no longer an academic question – but that the technical aspects of poetry and music are the interpretative means for whatever music and poetry might 'say' is not speculative. Techniques are at work as soon as we open our mouths. And in many cases they are shared or kindred techniques with those of music. In that sense it seems perfectly reasonable to talk about the 'musicality' of a particular set of words in a poem by Keats. What is potentially confusing though about doing so is that really we are talking about a quality inherent in poetry itself, from its origins, and not something borrowed from another art. And what, indeed, might we mean if we do talk about the 'musical' qualities of a poem? Well, I tentatively used the word, so I should first explain why.

I was talking about the words, 'Heard melodies are sweet, but those unheard / Are sweeter'. You will remember the last line of the Wordsworth stanza in Chapter 1 and the way we were able to see a remarkable number of sound linkages in the line, as well as an overall rhythmic patterning. We can find the same techniques at work here. Keats uses only nine words here, but the pattern of vowels and consonants is so packed and intricate that the syllable 'mel-' opening the key word 'melodies' is the only syllable that is left to its own devices. One sound – 'th' in 'those' – is similarly on its own. Grammatically, of course, this is directly related to 'melodies'. We might surmise that the effect of this, in fact, is to highlight the word 'melodies'. The linked sounds are 'heard'/ 'unheard'/'-er'; '-ies'/'sweet'/'sweeter'; 'are'/'are'; 'but'/'un-'; '-ose'/'-ies'; 'heard'/'-lod-'/'unheard'; '-eet'/'but'/'-eet'. Now it's easy to take this sort of thing too far. You may think I have already. But it's this quality in poetry that we often call 'music'. There is a music of vowels, and equally there is a music of consonants. I have picked out the same sounds, in a sense, the rhymes. But sound-changes also form patterns, almost physically felt patterns, as the mouth adjusts itself to utter the words of the sequence, and these also constitute a kind of music. Something of this sort is very strongly at work in the section of the Donne

sonnet I asked you about on page 12. It's probable that to achieve
a similar intricacy in instrumental music you would have to have
a number of instruments playing together. Also the swiftness
of Keats here, using a time-space of only nine syllables, is not
easy to achieve in music, which tends to sustain a single mood
or time signature or type of sound over much longer periods.
Poetry is extremely economic. Local textures in music are built on
repetition; those in poetry by variation.

In poetry then, effects of this kind are what we are prone to
call 'musical' but there is a better case perhaps for calling them
'poetic'. The term 'musical', in a way, is redundant or a misnomer
and arises from an account of music as well as of poetry too
greatly preoccupied with tone-colour – another odd term. It is a
constituent certainly. What I would want to emphasize as most
important in all this, however, is that the sounds establish a
pattern. This is why Eliot says 'Only by the form, the pattern, /
Can words or music reach / The stillness'.

There are two other uses for the word 'musical' I can think
of as applied to poetry. There is the highly technical one of
'singability'. Certain clenches of sound are near to unsingable. The
mouth just can't get round them. They may be highly poetic.
Look, for example, at Leontes's speech in *The Winter's Tale*:

> I' fecks!
> Why, that's my bawcock. What, hast smutch'd thy nose?
> They say it is a copy out of mine. Come, captain,
> We must be neat – not neat but cleanly, captain.
> And yet the steer, the heifer, and the calf
> Are all called neat. – Still virginalling
> Upon his palm? – How now, you wanton calf?
> Art thou my calf?[13]

This is rhythmically far too broken to be easily singable. It is far
too highly charged as well. Whereas Robert Herrick's

> Gather ye rosebuds while ye may,
>   Old Time is still a-flying:
> And this same flower that smiles to-day,
>   To-morrow will be dying.[14]

is much more singable, though the third line might give a few
problems, notably 'this same' and perhaps 'that smiles'. Try it.

One other type of musical verse occurs when a set of words
inevitably suggests an intonation pattern which corresponds to a
particular type of music or even a particular tune. This doesn't
happen often, but Eliot's lines in *The Waste Land*

O O O O that Shakespeherian Rag –
It's so elegant
So intelligent[15]

are an example.

These, then, are some particular instances where poetry and music may have an analogous relationship. But in this chapter I have wanted to make the much wider point that the arts share a preoccupation with form, pattern and rhythm; that in this way they respond to the condition of the world; that they respond less by imitation than by constructing, alongside the observed world, parallel rhythmic shapes; so that art is at one and the same time 'natural' and 'artificial', part of the world yet not that world itself. I have been concerned less with discussing particular techniques and more with providing a sense that the patterns the arts construct have a 'meaning' precisely by virtue of their being patterned and rhythmic and so echoing the wider conditions of our life.

In the next chapter we will get back to the techniques by means of which such a 'meaning' is constructed. So I'll leave you with some questions which will serve as the basis for our next discussion. **Can you apply the iambic pattern (ˣ ˋ) to Keats's 'Ode on a Grecian Urn' and to Wallace Stevens's 'Anecdote of the Jar' (page 24)? If you can, do they 'sound' the same or are there any differences you can locate? To start, you off, here is Keats's 'Ode on a Grecian Urn'.**

Thou still unravish'd bride of quietness,
   Thou foster-child of silence and slow time,
Sylvan historian, who canst thus express
   A flowery tale more sweetly than our rhyme:
What leaf-fring'd legend haunts about thy shape
    Of deities or mortals, or of both,
      In Tempe or the dales of Arcady?
    What men or gods are these? What maidens loth?
What mad pursuit? What struggle to escape?
    What pipes and timbrels? What wild ecstasy?

Heard melodies are sweet, but those unheard
   Are sweeter; therefore, ye soft pipes, play on;
Not to the sensual ear, but, more endear'd,
   Pipe to the spirit ditties of no tone:
Fair youth, beneath the trees, thou canst not leave
    Thy song, nor ever can those trees be bare;
      Bold Lover, never, never canst thou kiss,
Though winning near the goal – yet, do not grieve;
    She cannot fade, though thou hast not thy bliss,
      For ever wilt thou love, and she be fair!

Ah, happy, happy boughs! that cannot shed
  Your leaves, nor ever bid the Spring adieu;
And, happy melodist, unwearied,
  For ever piping songs for ever new;
More happy love! more happy, happy love!
  For ever warm and still to be enjoy'd,
    For ever panting, and for ever young;
All breathing human passion far above,
  That leaves a heart high-sorrowful and cloy'd,
    A burning forehead, and a parching tongue.

Who are these coming to the sacrifice?
  To what green altar, O mysterious priest,
Lead'st thou that heifer lowing at the skies,
  And all her silken flanks with garlands drest?
What little town by river or sea shore,
  Or mountain-built with peaceful citadel,
    Is emptied of this folk, this pious morn?
And, little town, thy streets for evermore
  Will silent be; and not a soul to tell
    Why thou art desolate, can e'er return.

O Attic shape! Fair attitude! with brede
  Of marble men and maidens overwrought,
With forest branches and the trodden weed;
  Thou, silent form, dost tease us out of thought
As doth eternity: Cold Pastoral!
  When old age shall this generation waste,
    Thou shalt remain, in midst of other woe
Than ours, a friend to man, to whom thou say'st,
  'Beauty is truth, truth beauty, – that is all
    Ye know on earth, and all ye need to know.'[16]

3. Patterns in Use: Before the Twentieth Century

I left you at the end of the last chapter pondering the scansion of two poems, in particular to see whether their metres were iambic. I hope that you will have found that Keats's 'Ode on a Grecian Urn' and Wallace Stevens's 'Anecdote of the Jar' do, in fact, present us with iambic patterns. To take the Keats first:

O Attic shape! Fair attitude! with brede
Of marble men and maidens overwrought.

Look at the rest of the poem in case these are the only iambic lines. Establish the dominant pattern, and note variations from it. And don't forget to do a syllable-count, line by line. Are there any lines which seem exceptions according to a syllable-count?

DISCUSSION

I think you will have found that Keats's basic approach is to present us with an iambic pattern in ten-syllabled lines – that is, iambic pentameters or iambic decasyllabics. To take the ten syllables first, there are a number of lines where you will have had to make a decision as to how to pronounce a word in respect of the number of its syllables. Assuming what seems clear, that Keats is aiming to write ten-syllabled lines, we will read 'historian' and 'mysterious' as three syllables not four, 'sensual' and 'adieu' as two not three, but 'deities' as three and 'Lead'st' and 'say'st' as one each, as Keats has indicated by contracting them. The line 'And, happy melodist, unwearied' then becomes the only one which might seem not to meet the ten-syllable mark. It's a syllable short, and this suggests, in the context of such regularity, that Keats wanted us to read 'unwearied' as four syllables. There are two ways of doing this. We could stretch out '-wear-', dwelling on it in a quantitative way, so that it has a longer time-value and therefore, the sense of an extra syllable – 'un-we-ar-ied'. Or we could notice that Keats rhymes 'unwearied' with 'shed' and pronounce it 'poetically' and not naturally as 'unwearièd'. Some editors do put an accent on the 'ed' to make sure we do and a degree of probability is on their side. It makes the line regular, both as to syllable-count and to iambic stress. I don't altogether like this way of doing it. I would prefer that we simply stretch out the second syllable of the word and so leave it sounding much as it does in speech. This way it would be both regular as to syllable-count and emotionally effective. The rhyme 'shed/unwearied' would then be a sort of eye-rhyme, that is a rhyme to the sight but not to the ear. Either way though the line can be understood as syllabically regular.

Now, as to the iambic pattern, you will have noticed that there are a lot of variations from it – though without endangering the basic rhythmic coherence of the whole poem. The poem is exceptionally tuneful and memorable, and a lot of the best tunes and most memorable bits – the bits people quote – are in fact playing tricks with the iambic. For example:

> Heard melodies are sweet, but those unheard
> Are sweeter; therefore, ye soft pipes, play on;

clearly responds to an iambic pattern but takes considerable liberties with it, twice in as many lines, according to my notation, packing pairs of heavy stresses together. Incidentally, you may well want to read 'ye soft pipes, play on' differently from me. Mine is only one way of rendering the subtle possibilities of these five syllables. They could be read 'ye soft pipes, play on' or 'ye soft pipes, play on'. My tendency in these matters of choice is to keep as close to the iambic pentameter as I sensibly can. I feel that the voice here is meditative and quiet, so I am a bit loath to give 'soft' and/or 'on' heavy stresses, but they are certainly capable of taking them in terms of sense. Indeed, it is as if a number of little tunes, with different highlights, are being presented to us simultaneously. But however we stress the words, a straightforward iambic reading is impossible. We might surmise that Keats is, in fact, deviating from the iambic so distinctly here in order to draw attention to the magisterial tone he is adopting. He is sticking his finger in the air and saying, 'This is important.' **Have you picked up any other places in the poem where he might equally be drawing attention to his words by deviating from a metrical norm?**

DISCUSSION

In a letter in 1820, Keats advised Shelley to 'load every rift of your subject with ore', to 'curb your magnanimity' and to settle for 'poetry' not 'purpose'. This seems to be suggesting deepening the texture of his writing by specifically poetic means – word-colour, widely drawn imagery and so on.[1] On the evidence of the 'Ode on a Grecian Urn', he might also have had in mind the use of shifting stress to heighten meaning, because he is himself a master of it. In this poem he is constantly inviting us to experiment in placing our emphases, loading the poem with heavier than normal stress and so slowing our reading down so that it becomes a poignant meditation. Most noticeable, of course, are the big moments like 'Beauty is truth, truth beauty' or 'Cold Pastoral!' but perhaps more revealing is a passage like

> What men or gods are these? What maidens loth?
> What mad pursuit? What struggle to escape?
> What pipes and timbrels? What wild ecstasy?

where the repeated, alerting 'What' jolts the iambic pattern without ever, in effect, displacing it. Notice too that Keats also plays with the quantities of closely related sounds, almost rhymes, in order to achieve variation: 'What $\bar{ma}$idens loth? / What $m\breve{a}d$ pursuit?'

Keats uses his punctuation to jolt the rhythm too. It's normal in a verse line to have a slight pause – called a caesura – usually placed towards the middle of the line. Its purpose is to accommodate the way the meaning falls to the rhythm of our breathing as we read. A caesura (Latin, 'cutting off' – from *caedere*, to cut) is a slightly less weighty pause than the one at the end of the line, which, in printed poetry, has an added visual weight and often heavier punctuation. Rhyme at the ends of lines adds weight to the pause there too. Keats uses caesura after caesura to make the reader feel his lines. If we take 'Of deities or mortals, ‖ or of both' or 'What mad pursuit? ‖ What struggle to escape?' as indicating a normal use of the caesura, then we find that Keats is also willing to write 'More happy love! ‖ more happy, ‖ happy love' or 'O Attic shape! ‖ Fair attitude! ‖ with brede' or 'Bold Lover, ‖ never, ‖ never canst thou kiss'. The effect of this on the metrical beat is again to jolt but not to displace it, rather to set up a complementary pattern within it. This, metrically speaking, is to 'load every rift . . . with ore'.

Consider the way you might, even must, read phrases like 'slow time', 'this folk, this pious morn', 'old age' and, of course, the deliberate slowing (because you can't read it fast) of 'leaf-fring'd legend'. You'll perceive, then, that Keats is exploiting a basic tension between what the iambic line leads us to expect and what the voice allows us to say. His meditative emphasis in these phrases, but also generally throughout the poem, is constantly overriding and yet confirming the metrical beat. It is confirmed because you could in most of the cases read the words following Desmond Graham's advice to exaggerate the beat, as iambic. But the sense of the words and the mood of the poem suggest that you don't. Experiment with the line 'That leaves a heart high-sorrowful and cloy'd'. Read it exaggerating the iambic pattern. Then read it again as you might wish to say it, attending to the meaning. My preferred reading would be, not the straight iambic:

That leaves a heart high-sorrowful and cloy'd,

but

That leaves a heart high-sorrowful and cloy'd,

The sense here is largely achieved by deliberate slowing and variation, arrived at metrically. Keats is constantly playing little tunes that flicker up and down above or, perhaps more accurately, within his metric.

I wrote earlier of Keats 'deviating' from the iambic, and this talk of little tunes above and within the metric seems to embody another effect that could be spoken of as 'deviation'. With some analysts, 'deviation' is, in fact, a favoured word to describe the way a poet modifies a basic, often received, metre – by deviating from it. Geoffrey Leech in his book *A Linguistic Guide to English Poetry* expressed the idea neatly and cast it more widely. He wrote:

> It is a very general principle of artistic communication that a work of art in some way deviates from norms which we, as members of society, have learnt to expect in the medium used . . . As a general rule, anyone who wishes to investigate the significance and value of a work of art must concentrate on the element of interest and surprise, rather than on the automatic pattern.[2]

To 'concentrate on the element of interest' means, for example, listening to the clarinet or trumpet solo as it stands out against a rhythm section in a jazz group. Much of my discussion of effects in Keats has drawn attention to elements which stand out, surprise or deviate in some way from an established norm. And so, as a general rule, concentrating on such elements of interest would seem to be good practice. **Can you see any hazards in too free a use of such an approach?**

DISCUSSION

Well, to begin with it doesn't strike me as the way the practitioner of an art is likely to talk about it, making a sharp distinction between 'automatic pattern' and 'the element of interest and surprise'. In the case of poets, they pay a lot of attention to their rhythms – the nearest thing to automatic pattern in verse. In 1920 Ezra Pound wrote:

> A rhythm unit is a shape; it exists like the keel-line of a yacht, or the lines of an automobile-engine, for a definite purpose, and should exist with an efficiency as definite as that which we find in yachts and automobiles.[3]

In jazz, a good rhythm section gives the basic drive which enables solo instruments to create their figures, always knowing exactly where they are in relation to the patterns of the music. As Jack Lemmon says when he sees Marilyn Monroe walking down the railway platform in *Some Like It Hot*, 'Get a load of that rhythm section.' A rhythm section is something to admire, the unit of energy which sustains the whole musical structure.

Equally, to 'concentrate on the element of interest and surprise' is to misread the way such surprise works and to mistake its purpose. In nineteenth-century landscape painting, a frequent device was to place a figure dressed in red in the foreground of a painting, a 'deviation' from the dominant colours of the scene. The idea of this device was to arrest attention and to focus the entire picture: to have a point which, by contrast, completed it, drawing its greens, browns, blues and greys together by a vivid oppositional stroke. This is deviation certainly. But its point is precisely to act as focus for the rest of the picture. It is not that the picture acts a foil to the stroke of red, but that the red makes clear, by contrast, the prevailing shapes and colours of the picture. The rhythm, and not just the single moment, is what the artist pursues, but – and this is important – the single moment is a key element in revealing the rhythm.

The case is even clearer in poetry. Poetry normally takes place on a single plane, the singularity implied by a succession of spoken words. It is unlike music, where, if drums, bass, piano and trumpet are playing simultaneously, we are conscious of a multi-layered effect where we can give precedence to a particular sound, which will normally but not invariably be the solo instrument. In poetry, such layering is not sonic so much as associational. The layers are of meanings that occur associationally when we hear a word – 'sky', 'green', 'ocean' or whatever. The only time that poetry can assume that musical relationship is when it is set to music or sung – that is, when it is itself used like another instrument. Rap is an interesting case because the voice is used precisely to allow the rhythm to dominate – that is, the deviation, the point of interest, is the automatic pattern, the rhythm. Recitative is a sort of minimalist rapping aimed to convey as much narrative information as possible with the least interruption from music.

In poetry, then, if deviation from a norm occurs, it will tend to confirm not to deny the automatic pattern. At the same time it is precisely within the automatic pattern that the deviation is located. And the best poetry is that which always allows us to feel the presence of the pattern, a pulse in the words, and yet is flexible enough to set up other tunes within it. As we read a Keats line, for example, the voice resonates with the stress we hear and the stress the metrical drive makes us infer:

> Thou, silent form, dost tease us out of thought
> As doth eternity: Cold Pastoral!

This limitation, that all effects in the words of a poem are simultaneous and placed in a one-by-one succession, is at the same time the area in which a poet's greatest skills are employed. We could not really grasp this without doing metrical analysis. I can say this with feeling. In the case of the 'Ode on a Grecian Urn', I had always realized how fine a poem it is. But not until I analysed it for this chapter, in a stream of light and heavy stresses, did I realize how amazingly accomplished it is.

Wallace Stevens equally sets up a metrical norm in 'Anecdote of the Jar'. The poem is on page 24. **What norm do lines 4 and 10 deviate from? Do you notice anything about the words which end the lines? Could you rhyme easily with them, do you think? And, looking at those sounds, are they echoed elsewhere in the poem other than at the ends of the lines? And what do you make of that?**

DISCUSSION

The basic line in 'Anecdote of the Jar' seems to have eight syllables (to be octosyllabic) and to be in iambic metre. Apart from lines 4 and 10, only the word 'slovenly' presents a problem to the earnest syllable-counter I hope you are by now. And the easy way to resolve that is to read it as 'slov'nly' (two syllables), which we probably do anyway. This gives the line eight syllables. That leaves line 4 with only four syllables and line 10 with only six.

Since I'm interested at this moment in eliciting basic patterns, I didn't ask why these two lines might be shorter. I suspect that most of us – me included – could supply only speculative answers. Speculation will be inclined to say that each of the lines enforces a silence in the poem at these points, both occurring at moments of revelation or realization within the poem. This will be to say that, in a quantitative sense, the missing syllables (four and two of them respectively if we suppose the octosyllabic norm) are to be supplied by us as metrically silent beats. Supplying beats like this is a way of regularizing lines so that quantitatively they are felt to occupy the same time-space; or, to speak musically, so that the beat-count is constant – a pause counting as one or more beats.

I am a bit uneasy with such a neat solution, regularizing the deliberately irregular. Rather I would want to allow the pause because Stevens has clearly written the line short for some such effect. But I would not wish to quantify it as if he had all along aimed at regularity. He has aimed at an irregular, not a regular effect, and by making it regular we should simply be stitching the whole thing up in a neat parcel. Besides, we are already expected to pause fairly heavily at the ends of both these lines. They both have full stops. And such a solution, by supplying invisible beats, is the thin end of a wedge which would enable us to rationalize every irregular break as regularity. A better way of putting it, I think, would be to say that, insofar as we notice the metrical variation – and I think in both these cases we do – the device draws attention to the words in the lines and their finality: an air of arriving at a point of realization. Short lines do often have this effect. It is as if at this point the poet is saying, 'Of this I have nothing more to say: my case rests.' Stevens doesn't want to pad the lines out into a spurious regularity.

And spareness is, of course, part of the theme of the poem – the 'gray and bare' jar giving form to shapeless nature. To emphasize this, Stevens has already used a rather spare form. The octosyllabic line is, or perhaps was, commonly used in ballads and hymns in various configurations but often involving short lines, say 8 6 8 6. So Stevens is gesturing towards such a past style. The octosyllabic line was often used for narrative too – telling stories with a popular edge, frequently at some length. This poem is short enough, but then it's only an 'Anecdote'. A line of this length,

not invariably but usually, invites a spare style. Adjectives, for
instance, take up space without forwarding the narrative that the
ballad and story-poem are intent upon, and so they tend to be
sparely used. They're more at home in the hymn. But even there
singability invites, even if it does not prescribe, simplicity. So once
again Stevens responds to the normal expectations of the ballad-
like form. All the forms I have mentioned were habitually rhymed
in straightforward ways – for example ABAB. Rhyme, of course,
was another way to make sure you kept it simple. If the need for a
rhyme comes at you on every eighth syllable so that you have only
seven syllables between rhymes, you need every one of those
syllables to take as much story-weight and forwarding drive as it
can. And, equally, you don't want to be looking for rhymes for,
let's say, 'scissors' too often.

This points to another thing about these four-beat metres:
that it is the oral and popular tradition in which they will have
often first come to birth – swift story-telling or songs where you
can pull the rhymes out of the air and keep it going, holding an
audience by your non-stop power of invention. In a twentieth-
century context, think of the rhyme-words of the blues: nearly
always simple, prescribed by the improvisatory mode and the
recurrence of basic but highly charged narrative situations. Now
Stevens doesn't give us a regular rhyme-scheme. It is another
departure, estranging himself from a tradition he is at the same
time gesturing towards. But, although the ideas are not simple, the
language is. And, at the points where we would expect rhymes,
the words he uses are very simple. Give a blues singer words like
'Tennessee', 'hill', 'it', 'wild', 'ground', 'everywhere' and you could
expect a blues – rhymes coming out of every bush in the wilderness to keep it going. But Stevens doesn't rhyme them. That's not
quite true. Across stanzas 3 and 4 he has 'air'/'everywhere'/'bare',
as if to say he could do it if he wanted to, and then the last line
brings us back to 'Tennessee', where we started from, enclosing
everything. Then there's 'hill' and 'hill'. The point here, with both
'Tennessee' and 'hill', is not that this is sharp rhyming. It isn't.
Stevens's technique is a much more elaborate example of the type
of aural echo that we saw at work in the last line of the Wordsworth stanza in Chapter 1. And, insofar as it involves direct
rhyme, it is a much more deliberately palpable example of the
kind of echoes we saw Keats using. Stevens, a highly conscious
craftsman, is repeating a set of sounds so that they net the poem
together – and so that we know they do. In order for what Stevens
wants to say to come across unmistakably, the poem must be both
spare and at the same time proclaim itself as a work of 'art',

something made. And there are other sounds distributed through the poem, notably 'round' (twice)/'surround'/'around'/'ground', which again estrange the poem from a traditional form in the way they are used and yet gesture towards it.

Notice how Stevens, whenever he wants to say 'jar', says it. Apart from 'it', he calls it nothing else. Keats, on the other hand, never calls an urn an urn – not once after the title. He has a fair number of tries – 'unravish'd bride', 'foster-child', 'Sylvan historian', 'Attic shape', 'Fair attitude', 'silent form', 'Cold Pastoral', 'a friend to man' – but he never quite makes it. Keats is going for an elaborate texture which accommodates, even relishes, this kind of verbal play, technically called 'variation'. Stevens is looking for simplicity, spareness. We could call 'The jar was round upon the ground' an internal rhyme, technically speaking, but, since it does not figure as part of a system using other internal rhymes, it looks much more as if Stevens is simply aiming to give his poem the benefits of rhyme without its formality. Similarly 'I placed a jar in Tennessee' gives the poem the air of a popular song, if a mildly surrealistic one, without actually committing Stevens to the full form of a song.

In 'Anecdote of the Jar' there seems, then, to be an interplay between a fully shaped and established aesthetic form (iambic octosyllabics; hints of rhyme-schemes; ballad, hymn or narrative patterns) and an unshaped form not yet fully realized (truncated lines; rhymes scattered around but not where they would normally occur; a strange sort of story). This we can deduce from an analysis of rhythm and more especially rhyme. It is a structural reading which coincides with the meaning that the words of the poem seem to suggest, the fully fashioned 'jar' giving form to 'the slovenly wilderness' which still sprawls around but is 'no longer wild'.

'Ode on a Grecian Urn' and 'Anecdote of the Jar' are two very different handlings of iambic pattern, separated one from another by more than a century. Together they indicate something of the remarkable flexibility of this particular rhythm. And they have also given us some sense of the ways in which poets can handle patterns of sound to reinforce meaning or, indeed, to increase our pleasure in the textures of the verse. Now we should look at the other major metrical patterns introduced briefly on page 4: trochaic, anapaestic and dactyllic metres. None of them is as vital to English verse as is the iambic. They are more difficult to write, and none could claim to work as closely with the habitual speech patterns of English as iambic can. The trochaic first: here is a piece of Robert Browning's 'One Word More', the poem with which he dedicated his book *Men and Women* (1855) to Elizabeth Barrett Browning. **Could you scan it, count the syllables and see whether there is a rhyme scheme?**

> What of Rafael's sonnets, Dante's picture?
> This: no artist lives and loves, that longs not
> Once, and only once, and for one only,
> (Ah, the prize!) to find his love a language
> Fit and fair and simple and sufficient –
> Using nature that's an art to others,
> Not, this one time, art that's turned his nature.
> Ay, of all the artists living, loving,
> None but would forego his proper dowry –
> Does he paint? he fain would write a poem –
> Does he write? he fain would paint a picture,
> Put to proof art alien to the artist's,
> Once, and only once, and for one only,
> So to be the man and leave the artist,
> Gain the man's joy, miss the artist's sorrow.[4]

DISCUSSION

Did you get hold of the trochaic pattern?

What of Rafael's sonnets, Dante's picture?

It is remarkably regular, in fact, and by now your expectations of the flexibility of a metrical pattern as a poet actually uses it will readily take on board variations within it which do not distract from the onward rhythmic drive – for example, the line 'Fit and fair and simple and sufficient'. The lines are again ten syllables, and there are no rhymes. This a type of English blank verse. I say 'a type' because blank verse is normally in iambic, not trochaic, pentameter. Trochaic verse is not easy to sustain in English. This is the only time Browning wrote trochaic blank verse. Elsewhere in the poem he says, interestingly,

> Take these lines, look lovingly and nearly,
> Lines I write the first time and the last time.

It sounds as if Browning is saying that the trochaic metre is more trouble than it's worth or, at least, a bit special, not to be used too often. Bearing in mind what an extraordinary inventiveness Browning had, this may help us to realize why such an apparently simple change, the reversal of the iambic foot (ˣˋ to ˋˣ), is so little used in English. In fact, the trochee's major importance is as a widely adopted variant within the iambic pattern itself.

Now look at the line endings in the piece from 'One Word More'. What do you notice about the stress? How many syllables have the majority of the last words of the lines? Does this give the lines a particular atmosphere?

DISCUSSION

It naturally follows from the use of a trochaic metre that most of the lines will end on a light stress. This in turn means that most of the lines will end with a two-syllabled word. A rhythm like this, where the heavy stress precedes the light stress, is often called a 'falling' rhythm, as opposed to a 'rising' rhythm like the iambic. But, to be honest, this rise or fall is pretty difficult to pick up by listening to it, except at the beginning and the end of the lines. Obviously the bit in the middle is actually the same. It all depends where you start counting. For instance, we could turn the trochaic pentameter

What of Rafael's sonnets, Dante's picture?

into an iambic hexameter (twelve syllables) by adding two syllables:

And what of Rafael's sonnets, Dante's picture there?

and leave the body of the line intact, but having reversed the metre. To detect a falling metre, then, you really need the trochee to close the line. Traditionally this type of closure on an unstressed syllable is called a 'feminine ending'. In iambic verse it is an occasional effect only; in trochaic writing it sets the tone.

What that tone is – 'atmosphere' I called it when I asked the question – is harder to say. A final trochee is often used to achieve a 'dying fall', a lingering at the end of the line. The final syllable seems to be suspended in the pause which we tend to observe after a line has ended, like the resonating of a musical note long after it is first struck. As a very good example of this effect, notice how Andrew Marvell uses the falling rhythm of the word 'Impossibility' in 'The Definition of Love':

> My Love is of a birth as rare
> As 'tis for object strange and high:
> It was begotten by despair
> Upon Impossibility.[5]

This is the more effective because the falling rhythm is extended through a long sequence of light stresses – 'Impossibility' – and it is used to close an otherwise impeccable iambic quatrain. The effect is strengthened, in other words, by contrast. Browning achieves similar effects in 'Aye, of all the artists living, lòvĭng', in 'Once, and only once, and for one ònlȳ' and in 'Gain the man's joy, miss the artist's sòrrŏw.'

But just as Marvell's effect was reinforced by the metrical context in which he used it, so Browning's meaning depends on his use of a much wider set of effects than simply the way he ends his lines. Most of us, for example, have a set of associations with words like 'only', 'loving', and 'sorrow' which will contribute strongly to an atmosphere of 'dying fall'. On the whole, then, my question as to 'atmosphere' is very difficult to answer. But we should certainly watch out for any special metrical effects, just to make sure we don't make fools of ourselves when we think we have located them.

While we are talking about trochees, it's noticeable that, in English verse at least, trochaic rhyme is often used in comic situations. Consider the following lines from Thackeray's 'The Sorrows of Werther':

> Charlotte, having seen his body
> Borne before her on a shutter,
> Like a well-conducted person,
> Went on cutting bread and butter.[6]

This is clearly comic, and the rhyme 'shutter'/'bread and butter' contributes strongly to the comedy. **Can you see how we would test the assertion that it is the trochaic nature of the line endings here ('body' and 'person' are also trochees) that establishes the comic tone?**

DISCUSSION

Well, by far the best way is to rewrite the passage maintaining the rhyme-sounds and rhythms or whatever other aspect of the verse is under discussion but changing the tone. Doing this has two virtues. One is that it usually shows that a rhythm or a particular sound or rhyme carries with it no automatic effects. Everything depends on context. The other is that it proves to yourself that you too can write – and enjoy writing – trochees, iambs, anapaests or whatever. It familiarizes you with them and converts mysteries into abilities. It's easy, too, because you have a precise model (in this case from Thackeray) in front of you.

In preparing for this book, one of my most cheerful moments was testing the validity of Derek Attridge's detailed account of these lines from W. H. Auden:

Victor looked up at the mountains,
The mountains all covered with snow;
Cried; 'Are you pleased with me, Father?'
And the answer came back; 'No'.

Victor came to the forest,
Cried; 'Father, will she ever be true?'
And the oaks and the beeches shook their heads
And they answered; 'Not to you.'

Attridge comments, 'The chilling finality of the replies is conveyed
in part by the shift in the last line of each stanza from a light and
rapid movement created by double offbeats to a weightier alternation of beats and single offbeats (a change which in the second
stanza begins in the nightmarish headshakes of the penultimate
line).'[7] He then tests what he says by changing the rhythms of the
last two lines, and to some extent this does lessen the effect. But
what he should do is to maintain the rhythms, since it is these, he
suggests, that produce the effect, and to change instead the words
which fill up the rhythms and see, then, if the rhythms maintain
the effect. When I changed the words, the verses came out like
this:

Victor booked up at 'The Fountains',
'The Fountains' at Bourton-on-Stow;
Asked; 'Will you come with me, Peter?'
And the answer came back; 'No'.

Victor went to the florists,
Said; 'Roses, can they ever be blue?'
And the man at the counter shook his head
And he answered; 'Not a clue.'

It is as well to take account of Attridge's cautionary phrase 'in
part', qualifying his case, but none the less it seems clear that it is
the particular words used by Auden and the context he creates
that most establish his meaning. Metres seldom have automatic
effects. They are a vehicle, an algebra, carrying many meanings.

In the case of Thackeray's trochees and his rhymes, suppose
we rewrite them using the same metre and the same rhyme-
sounds, but change the tone? Here's one way of doing it.

Hardened warriors saw his body
Borne before them on a shutter,
Like an offering raised to heaven,
Strangling thoughts no man could utter.

What is the difference between these lines and Thackeray's?

DISCUSSION

The first thing to say is that they're not so funny – at least I hope they're not. I've kept the metre pretty much as Thackeray had it, and I've kept the rhyme-sounds. However, since I have chosen to describe an heroic scene – a dead warrior being borne from battle on an improvised bier – there's no way I could really hang on to the phrase 'bread and butter'. Getting rhymes for 'shutter' isn't impossible, but it's not one of the first words you would look for if you were trying to keep things easy. The chief difficulty, as you will well see, was to find a context in which a body being borne on a shutter would seem normal. Having fixed on heroic death in battle, I then added to it the religious image – the man raised up in death – and the idea of a grief which could not find expression. All this high seriousness is a kind of 'sacred parody', just as hymn-writers, from early Christian times on, have often used popular songs as a basis for their hymns. The point is that the 'algebra' of the tune or the metre will usually take the change. Folk-song is the same: one tune is capable of carrying many sets of words. There is nothing inherently comic in either Thackeray's metre or his rhyme. The comedy is in the use Thackeray puts them to.

So much for feminine endings in trochaic metre. I want you now to consider a couple of other devices that Browning uses in the lines from 'One Word More'. These are not to do with trochaic metre as such, but they do help to explain how he individualizes his use of a strict metre. He has been very precise in his use both of trochaic stress and of ten-syllable count, but nevertheless the voice that seems to control both these structural devices is Browning's own. **First, what do you notice about lines like these?**

> Put to proof art alien to the artist's,
> Once, and only once, and for one only,

How characteristic are they of the whole passage?

DISCUSSION

These lines have an unusual amount of alliteration – the chiming together of the initial letters of words. And they are characteristic of the whole passage. In fact, I chose these two lines in particular, because they show some especially subtle types of alliteration. The words 'art'/'artist's', 'Once'/'once'/'one', 'only'/'only' are examples of strict alliteration, not to mention identity. Without stretching it too far, we can say they are rhyming, since they function as

rhymes do, binding the passage together in a net of sound. It's a
bit of a quibble not to include 'Put' and 'proof' as examples of
strict alliteration. 'Prude' and 'proof' would be strict, but most
poets would welcome the chance of a little variation while maintaining the most part of the alliterative sound being used. But the
sequences 'art'/'alien'/'artist's' and, even more so, 'only'/'once'/
'one'/'only' involve a sort of alliteration for the eye, visual more
than sonic. It's at least interesting that Browning is here writing
about exchanges between artists of the eye (painters) and artists
primarily of the ear (poets), but I'm sure that's only a happy
coincidence. Not at all coincidental, though, is Browning's repeated use of parallel constructions, often reinforced by alliteration. **Can you find some examples of parallel constructions? And
what is their effect, do you think?**

DISCUSSION

There are lots of them. 'Rafael's sonnets, Dante's picture', 'fit and
fair', 'Using nature that's an art to others', 'Does he paint? . . .
Does he write? . . .' and so on. Some alliterate, some do not. Their
first effect is, of course, just as with alliteration, to tighten the
structure. Again it is a rhyme-like device. At heart, too, it is
metrical. Hebrew poetry is based on parallel structures, as illustrated by the Psalms in the Old Testament. And the Psalms have
been metrically fruitful for a number of poets writing in English,
including Christopher Smart in the eighteenth century, William
Blake and Walt Whitman in the nineteenth and Allen Ginsberg in
the twentieth.[8] In 'One Word More', the parallelisms act as a kind
of metrical counterpoint to the trochaic rhythm. Parallelism of
this kind is in no way implied by the trochaic line, but, as an
intellectual device, it can be laid over it, in this case as a persistent
though dexterous tune. And it is undoubtedly an appropriate tune,
precisely because of the processes of exchange in the arts and
artists that Browning is talking about. It is the thought, and not
simply the form that the thought is given, that has a parallel
shape. We will come back to this distinction when we talk about
couplets in Chapter 6.
     Finally, a brief look at anapaests and dactyls. **Read aloud
these lines from Byron's 'The Destruction of Sennacherib':**

The Assyrian came down like the wolf on the fold,
And his cohorts were gleaming in purple and gold.[9]

**How do they scan? And now, some lines from Thomas Hood's
'The Bridge of Sighs':**

Touch her not scornfully;
Think of her mournfully,
  Gently and humanly;
Not of the stains of her,
All that remains of her
  Now is pure womanly.[10]

How about those?

DISCUSSION

I scan the Byron like this:

The Assyrian came down like the wolf on the fold,
And his cohorts were gleaming in purple and gold;

You will notice that I have scanned 'came down', whereas speech
would suggest 'came down'. But the drive of the metre is so
insistent that it will scarcely allow speech rhythm to interfere with
it. There is no counterpoint, only the gallop. This is an anapaestic
metre ($^{xx\`}$). With twelve syllables to the line, it's the anapaestic
hexameter.

I would scan the Hood equally insistently:

Touch her not scornfully;
Think of her mournfully.

This is a dactyllic metre ($^{\`xx}$). Remember my way of thinking of
this: an anapaest is a stretched iamb, stretched by an additional
light syllable; and a dactyl is a stretched trochee, stretched by an
additional light syllable.

As elements in English scansion, anapaests and dactyls are
important in two ways. First, there are a number of poems written
in these metres. The examples you have been scanning are from
two celebrated ones. But a general sense of the workings of poetry
will readily tell us that these are fairly special metres, used for
particular effects, sometimes for the helluva it. If we try to describe these effects – stately, elegiac, racy, energetic, tripping and
so on – we can usually come up with a parody that reverses all
those values, and we are back to concepts of association and
context as better explanations of what happens in any particular
poem. But, undeniably, such special metres establish the poem as a
made thing, a network. Metre is creating that sense we have of the
particular form. The sombre drumbeat element in 'The Bridge of
Sighs' is what creates the poem as, if you like, an 'occasion'.

The other usefulness of these metrical patterns is as a way of achieving local variations in iambic or trochaic verse, where an additional light stress before or after a heavy stress will give an anapaestic or dactyllic feel to the line. Anapaests are particularly good for incorporating the many English phrases which model like 'on the cliff, in the air', as we noticed with the lines from Wordsworth in Chapter 1. Dactyls are very good for incorporating three-syllabled adverbs, as the lines from Hood indicate. But, unless such variations are used very frequently in a poem, there is often an easier way of describing them – as trochaic reversals within an iambic line, for example. A poem like Charles Wolfe's 'The Burial of Sir John Moore':

> Not a drum was heard, not a funeral note,
> As his corpse to the rampart we hurried;
> Not a soldier discharged his farewell shot
> O'er the grave where our Hero we buried.[11]

is usefully seen as anapaestic with iambic variation. It sounds as if it has been written to that fashion. Another tricksy and celebrated Irish poem, Francis Sylvester Mahony's 'The Bells of Shandon', seems to me better described as iambic with anapaestic variation:

> With deep affection and recollection
> I often think of the Shandon bells,
> Whose sounds so wild would, in days of childhood,
> Fling round my cradle their magic spells.[12]

Again the metre, which is capable of imitation – it breeds true – is sufficiently defined and deliberate to merit description in these traditional terms.

In the next chapter I want to look at some of the methods used in twentieth-century poetry. In the three chapters so far, we have reviewed the main English metres in use from the sixteenth to the beginning of the twentieth century as well as a range of ways of varying them, employing quantity, counterpoint and so on. We have looked at rhyme and a variety of rhyme-like devices. We have also looked at rhyme and rhythms not simply as technical features of verse but as ones which by their very nature imply a meaning. This meaning has to do with the importance in the world, in art and in our lives of rhythm and relationship, an importance of which the forms of poetry are an integral part.

4. Patterns in Use: Twentieth-Century Verse Methods

So far we have examined a variety of rhythmic structures commonly in use through four centuries of English poetry. This variety has been presented through a light description, using traditional terms – iambs and trochees and the rest. Central to what has been developed is an idea of rhythm and rhyme as establishing a series of relational bonds in sound, stress and line-length which together stabilize the existence and therefore the meaning of the poem.

At the end of Chapter 2 we looked at three pieces of poetry which had in common the image of the vase or jar. Two, by John Keats and Wallace Stevens, were in iambic metre, and became the basis for our continuing investigation of the iambic in Chapter 3. Now I want you to look at the metric of the third piece, part of T. S. Eliot's *Four Quartets*. You will find the lines on page 25. I want to use them to introduce our discussion of twentieth-century verse methods. Can you find an iambic pattern in them, or, for that matter, a trochaic, anapaestic or dactyllic one? As usual, write out the passage using the scansion marks. One more thing: do you remember the account of the caesura – the midline break – when we were discussing Keats? Mark the caesuras in Eliot's lines, thus: ‖ .

DISCUSSION

This is the way I would like to do it:

Words move, ‖ music moves
Only in time; ‖ but that which is only living
Can only die. ‖ Words, after speech, reach
Into the silence. ‖ Only by the form, the pattern,
Can words ‖ or music reach
The stillness, ‖ as a Chinese jar still
Moves perpetually ‖ in its stillness.

The first thing to say is that, whatever this is, it's not iambic, nor any of the other metres we've so far come across. An exaggerated reading, such as Desmond Graham suggests, will have a very rocky time with this. The second thing to say is that you may well disagree with some of my stress-values. To tell the truth, I hope you do, because particularly with lines 2 and 3, I have been very idiosyncratic. I have wanted to read these lines as almost brooding, inward, and so have played down their potential for heavy stresses. This shows especially in my wish to give no heavy stress to the second and third occurrences of 'only'. At the same time, with the first and the fourth (in line 4), I have given the word emphatic stress: 'Only'. I have to say that logic is against me. Logic suggests as the preferred reading 'Only in time; but that which is only living / Can only die' and it's far safer to stay with that. My interpretation depends on a sense that the flatter we can read these lines about a life in time, as compared with its projection beyond time ('after speech ... the silence ... the stillness'), the more we will strike a jaded world-weary tone, relieved only by the heavily stressed finality of 'die'. But this is interpretation. There is a story that W. H. Auden visited Eliot one day and found him playing patience. 'What are you doing that for?' asked Auden. 'Well, I suppose it's the nearest thing to being dead,' answered Eliot.[1] It's something of that spirit – or lack of it – that I'm trying to see here. ('What are you doing?' 'Only living; only dying.') Another place where it would be easy to disagree with me, is in line 6, which could well be read 'The stillness, as a Chinese jar still', not as I have read it, with a heavy stress on 'still'.

This sort of problem occurred in much the same terms in our previous analyses. Sometimes we've been in doubt about the way to read something and found that our spoken stress did not always coincide with the metrical drive. Instead, reading it aloud effected a kind of counterpoint with the metre, and this, in turn, gave interest and variety to the line without destroying its pulse. In an iambic verse, 'Can only die' would have appeared as 'Can only

dìe' – the assumed underlying beat – but in performance we could
have read 'Càn ònlẙ dìe' or 'Càn ŏnlẙ dìe' or 'Căn ŏnlẙ dìe' and
added the excitement of a variety of potential meanings as a
counterpoint simultaneous with the assumed metric. But in a verse
which does not have regularity based on a steady alternation or
repetition, the rhythm we read could, perhaps, best be understood
as the rhythm that exists. The counterpoint then, if that exists, is
not with an assumed metre, but rather with a range of possible
meanings. The stability of the verse is not a sonic stability which
we play games with, but a stability of ambiguities where we
choose one meaning, indicated by stress, knowing that other
possible meanings exist, also indicated by stresses, recognized and
potential, but which we have chosen, on this occasion, not to use.
The economy in the present lines is not as it was with Keats, in
containing in the one set of metrically arranged words both more
than one rhythm and more than one meaning: rather, it is in
layering several meanings in the same words and choosing one
now, knowing that tomorrow we would be entitled to choose
another.

   In Eliot's verse, it is difficult to exclude or determine meanings on metrical evidence alone. In that sense, it is a very flexible
medium. And yet we cannot avoid feeling that a rhythm of some
kind – and one more determined than that in ordinary speech –
is at work in these lines. I want now to try to establish what
constructs that rhythm, working, as it were, from the first prin-
ciples of simple analysis. **Could you look again at the passage, and
count the syllables in each line as well as the number of heavy
stresses in each of them?**

DISCUSSION

The stresses are, of course, debatable, but in my reading there are
either three or four heavy stresses in all of the lines (4 3 4 4 3 4 3).
The syllables are not debatable but line by line show a wide,
though not excessive, range (5 12 9 13 6 9 9). This range indicates
that, while there is a wide divergence in line-length, there is a
convergence in the number of heavy stresses. There is, by the
same token, a wide divergence in the number of light stresses
(1 9 5 9 3 5 6). Now, as an experiment, adjust the passage so
as to achieve something nearer equality in the line lengths. It
will perhaps help you if you first total up the number of syllables
in the entire passage and divide that number by the number of
lines.

DISCUSSION

The passage contains 63 syllables in seven lines, so, if Eliot were trying to write lines which were syllabically equal here, he would go for a nine-syllabled line. (My first impulse, doing anything like this, is to think admiringly about how much the poet has said in so few syllables. We quite often manage to say very little in 63 syllables, or 600 for that matter.) You will have found that adjusting the passage to nines isn't difficult. Three of the lines are already nines. To make such an adjustment you should try to respect natural breaks in the sense as much as you can in determining where your rearranged lines begin and end. I would make only two moves, shifting the words 'Only in time' from line 2 to line 1 and 'the pattern' from line 4 to line 5. This gives a syllable-count of 9 8 9 10 9 9 9. (I am reading 'perpetually' as four syllables, not five, which is debatable – probably undesirable – but doesn't unduly affect what happens.) It also gives quite a solid piece of writing:

> Words move, music moves only in time;
> But that which is only living
> Can only die. Words, after speech, reach
> Into the silence. Only by the form,
> The pattern, can words or music reach
> The stillness, as a Chinese jar still
> Moves perpetually in its stillness.

Now why didn't Eliot write this, do you think? He could quite easily; it accommodates the sense well, and he clearly hasn't got anything against nine-syllabled lines. The easiest way to answer this question, I think, is to count the heavy stresses in each line of the nine-syllable version, making sure you don't, of course, change the individual stress values you assigned the words when you analysed Eliot's own lines.

DISCUSSION

Those of you who are less simple-minded than me, and more mathematically acute, will not be struck with the force of revelation when you find that there is now an extreme disparity in the number of heavy stresses in the lines – between the most and the least, that is. With my readings, the distribution is now 6 1 4 2 4 4 3. To take the most extreme cases, the new line 1 carries six heavy stresses in nine syllables and the new line 2 carries one in eight as against 4 and 3 in my preferred reading of Eliot's actual version. It is possible, therefore, to argue that

Eliot's lines 1 and 5 are so short in order to keep the number of heavy stresses to a norm of three or four to the line, and lines 2 and 4 are so long in order to achieve the same norm. In other words, Eliot is not too much worried about the number of syllables he puts in each line, but he is concerned to strike a rough equality in his heavy stresses. It equally follows that he doesn't mind about the number of light stresses. Eliot's regularity then – the rhythm we are conscious of – is based on a rough equality of heavy stresses – three or four to the line. At this point, nothing else – at least, nothing that can be handled in this numerical way – seems to establish that rhythm.

But there are other elements that help to structure the verse, to press pattern upon it. **Remember the caesuras? We can bring them into play now. What effect do they have?**

DISCUSSION

The caesuras aren't difficult. Eliot mostly marks them with punctuation of his own, a roughly centrally placed comma, semi-colon or full stop. Even the lines not clearly divided invite us to pause somewhere. So I notated the last three lines for example

Can words ‖ or music reach
The stillness, ‖ as a Chinese jar still
Moves perpetually ‖ in its stillness.

As to the effect of these pauses, that is more difficult to specify. But I think they lay down another structure of phrasing on the lines. If we observe the caesuras, we read with two sets of pauses – in the middle and at the end of the lines – each set weighted slightly differently. And also something happens round about the caesura. In my estimate, caesuras occur after 'move', 'time', 'die', 'silence', 'words', 'stillness' and 'perpetually', and the effect of the caesura is to put a little more emphasis on these words. The caesuras, then, specify the contours of our breathing, but also of our mental processes. Eliot is, in fact, taking advantage of an element in the structure of most verse: that the line divides naturally into two half-lines. He simply makes sure we cannot ride roughshod over this division and so gives it a little more metrical weight. He adds balance to his lines too, in that there is no half-line without at least one heavy stress. The caesuras, then, assist the rhythmic unity that is unmistakable in the writing.

By now we are used to looking for the rhyme-like verbal patternings that occurred, for example, in the lines we looked at from Keats, Stevens and Browning. **Can you see anything like that in Eliot's lines?**

DISCUSSION

If you spend a bit of time drawing rings round the individual words in the passage and then adding lines to connect them with words that have similar sounds, you will finish up just as you would have with our earlier quotations, with something like a spider's web, a network of connections. There are the parallels you can't miss; 'move'/'moves', 'Only'/'only'/'only'/'Only', 'Words'/'Words'/'words', 'speech'/'reach', 'music'/'music', 'stillness'/'still'/'stillness'. But there are also sequences using the same vowels distributed over several lines, like 'time'/'die'/'silence'/ 'by'/'Chinese'. Then notice how the crucial word 'pattern' has its elements taken up and distributed in 'perpetually in its stillness', a phrase which itself echoes along its whole length. This is vowel- and consonant-music which extends from full rhyme to the most delicate of effects.

Nearly all poetry will, on examination, reveal such sonic relationships. They are a condition both of a language – its propensity to use particular sounds and so on – and the way we will use it – with respect to our physical capabilities, habit, the constraints and requirements of memory and our degree of delight in it. Everything about language promotes and requires pattern, and poetry merely reflects and makes more intense that tendency and need. You may well be sceptical as to the degree of deliberation involved in the creation of such networks of sound, and you would be right. Obviously some of the effects are deliberate, the repetitions, for example. Others are the products of a choice which may often be, in part or even wholly, unconscious. It no doubt did not occur to Eliot to write 'perpetually in its static condition', but, if it did, he wouldn't have. Conscious choice is thinking of it and rejecting it. Unconscious choice which, I would maintain, is a poet's greatest skill or gift is thinking of 'stillness' in the first place, not only because of its sense, but also because it matches with a scheme of sound already at play in the creating mind. I am sceptical of people talking about 'liquid *l*s building up a sense of peace' and stuff like that, but of the pattern I am entirely convinced. However different Eliot's metric may be from the previous tradition, these verbal effects, drawing the whole structure together, are entirely traditional.

I have already suggested that Eliot's line was flexible. In many ways, it was a fresh flexibility in English verse, born, in part, from a wish to avoid the iambic pentameter. **As regards the distribution of stresses, how do you see this flexibility working? What can Eliot do metrically that Keats, for example, is not permitted to do by his metric?**

DISCUSSION

Undoubtedly the Eliot line is flexible, but, nonetheless, it exerts its own order, giving him a constant but not slavish stress. It gives him no anxiety about bunching heavy stresses together. In other words, he feels himself free to write 'Words move, music moves' (four out of five of the stresses are heavy). But then Keats had felt no anxiety about bunching heavy stresses in the way he used the iambic. It was part of loading every rift with ore.

On the whole, bunching heavy stresses as an occasional device in English poetry isn't a great problem, because its effect is to strengthen the latent rhythm, to add colour and emphasis to it, rather than to sink it under an undue weight. So Eliot can't be thinking of changing the basic patterns of English metre (which is what he did) in order to load every rift with ore. Rather, he wanted to thin his ore out a bit. It's the unstressed or, as I would say, the lightly stressed syllables that require the change. With a line like this, Eliot had no anxiety about lightly stressed syllables. He could write 'but that which is only' or 'into the silence. Only by the' or 'stillness, as a' or 'perpetually in its' without turning a metrical whisker or, more important, without involving the line in a false iambic echo. His chosen (and self-invented) metre gives him the rules or, to use his word, the 'pattern' for just such low-key utterances, the inertia of speech, within which the high colour can take its natural, not enforced, shape. In this often slightly flattened style, the sudden bit of bravura – 'Words, after *speech, reach*', for example – is not outrageous or gauche but oddly welcome, a sort of bracing shock. Keats had no particular way to bunch light stresses, certainly not in the iambic, because regular or alternating metres sweep up lightly stressed syllables into their patterns, lending them a stress they might not otherwise possess. But then one can surmise that he didn't feel a particular need for runs of lightly stressed syllables.

On the other hand, the flexibility Eliot was after was not to engage with high colour but to disengage from it. In a way, we might say he wanted a poetry that was less 'poetic'. He thought, for example, that

> to have the virtues of good prose is the first and minimum require-
> ment of good poetry ... The development of blank verse in the
> hands of Shakespeare and some of his contemporaries was the work
> of adapting a medium which to begin with was almost intractably
> poetic, so that it could carry the burdens and exhibit the subtleties of
> prose; and they accomplished this before prose itself was highly
> developed.[2]

This is the first time we have encountered the idea that poetry might learn something from prose. Following Eliot, it would seem that poetry might benefit by taking on some of the 'burdens' of prose – the tasks it has to perform – and gain some of its subtleties. In a way, I am suggesting that some of those subtleties are to do with a flexible, unassuming but ever-present rhythm, and that is less to do with the distribution of heavy stresses than with the utilization of light stresses. **A question then. What tasks can prose rhythms be said to perform well? I say 'prose rhythms' so that we don't lose touch with the question of rhythm itself. But the question won't be materially different if you think of the uses that prose has habitually been put to. These will indicate what the rhythms have been used for.**

DISCUSSION

The French poet Paul Valéry once said that he could never write a novel because he could not write, 'The countess went out at five o'clock.' This is the poet rejecting one of the tasks – the 'burdens' – of prose. Deciding not to write a treatise on logic or a book on metre is another. Prose has become an all-purpose medium, used skilfully by scientists, lawgivers, historians and vicars as well as novelists. In some ways, prose might be seen as usurping some of the ground that poetry had itself once occupied, in that in an oral society which remembered its knowledge, its laws, history and liturgies in chants, without recourse to writing, those chants were poetic, heavily rhythmic, the rhythms and their intricacies of sound assisting the memory and making special the knowledge they preserved and, indeed, the type of language they used. It's noticeable, even now, that poetry is more easily remembered than prose, and this is to do with rhyme and rhythm, which act as so many points of reminder, tying our minds closely into the structures of the words. With the advent of writing, memory becomes less important, because we can save the knowledge outside the mind, in a book or a vault. And so the rigours of the poem can be relaxed into the open, less regulated, structures of prose. That doesn't mean that these less regulated rhythms are easier to write, incidentally. On the contrary, there's a good case to be made that they're harder, because you are on your own a bit more. I would settle for 'as hard'. At the same time, prose can accommodate fine gradings of information and preoccupy itself with content. A treatise on logic is an argument to be countered by another argument. A chanted genealogy is an act, telling a people who and what it is.

Eliot, I think, felt that poetry in his time had lost this sense of quasi-sacral act. Its rhythms were repetitions, not explorations, the outmoded preserve of imprecisely perceived feelings. Nor were the rhythms and patterns of poetry used to deal with society's compelling issues. This was now the function of prose. What poetry needed was to be recharged with 'the virtues of good prose' – primarily, a flexible but palpable rhythm – so that it could take back the large subjects that prose now explored, that poets once had and that Eliot does in *The Waste Land* and *Four Quartets*. It was a way to resist the dated seductions of iambic metre and, in Ezra Pound's phrase, to 'Make it new'.[3]

We tend, in our preoccupation with stress in our language, to see avoidance of the iambic as being achieved by a less regimented distribution of heavy stresses. But the augmentation or reduction of heavy stresses was never a real difficulty in English verse. Poetry needed – and the virtues of good prose showed how to go about it – a way of handling runs of minimally stressed syllables so that they remained 'poetic', integral to the rhythm of the lines, and weren't just perceived as so much infill between heavy stresses. In some sense, Eliot's revolution in metre can be thought of as democratic: the unnoticed light stresses brought to emancipation, like so many Prufrocks nervously thrust into the limelight, heroes for our time.

I use this image of democracy not as idle flourish, but because the modern sea-change in rhythm had been anticipated in America by Walt Whitman when, in 1855, he published *Leaves of Grass*, speaking 'the pass-word primeval' and giving 'the sign of democracy'.[4] Whitman's line is not the same as Eliot's, but it is as released from the constraints of iambic and is even more characterized by the free use of lightly stressed syllables. Try to put a regular scansion on these lines, for example:

> The spotted hawk swoops by and accuses me, he
>   complains of my gab and my loitering.
> I too am not a bit tamed, I too am untranslatable,
> I sound my barbaric yawp over the roofs of the world.[5]

It's impossible, but they are powerfully rhythmic. Eliot may have been less passionate for democracy than Whitman, to put it mildly, but he was, in origin at least, just as American. I want to suggest – and in this book so far it is a new kind of statement, less technical than cultural – that it is not accidental that the main poets of our century who together changed the rhythms of English poetry were all American: T. S. Eliot, Ezra Pound and William

Carlos Williams.[6] Consciously or unconsciously, they had behind them the example of Walt Whitman. And, for the most part consciously, all had to come to terms with an emerging, potentially powerful but, up to then, sparse culture – a culture that each had either to reject or to help build. As poets, any building would begin first by constructing an appropriate rhythm and language. Eliot and Pound may have worked largely in Europe and within European traditions, but I would suggest that they brought to those traditions American minds and needs.

So much for suggestion. In the next two chapters I will be making connections between changes in poetic methods and means and wider cultural changes within the English tradition. Change in poetic method is deeply involved with social and cultural change and, in studying it, we are never just looking at the mechanics of sound or arbitrary literary techniques. To conclude this chapter then I want to look at two important twentieth-century developments in poetic method, one American and one English, where such cultural contexts may be involved.

In his writing, William Carlos Williams sought 'the American grain', specifically American metres, language and forms to engage with a specifically American locale.[7] In much of his work he came up with solutions like this, the first part of 'The Yellow Flower':

What shall I say, because talk I must?
    That I have found a cure
        for the sick?
I have found no cure
    for the sick
        but this crooked flower
which only to look upon
    all men
        are cured. This
is that flower
    for which all men
        sing secretly their hymns
of praise. This
    is that sacred
        flower![8]

There's not much point in counting syllables or stress here, except perhaps to emphasize that the lines are constructed in a very spare way so that they don't get out of hand as Whitman's can. They can be contained easily by the eye, by the ear and by the breath. This leads to the question I'd like you to start off with. **Where in the lines would you want to place the caesuras, if anywhere at all?**

DISCUSSION

Although I think this is the right place to start, it is a bit of a sneaky question. In the first line there is a nice fat caesura – 'What shall I say, ‖ because talk I must?' – and that could lead you to seeing every possibility of a pause, however imperceptible, as trying to be a caesura. But, in fact, I think there are only two other caesuras within the words of the lines themselves. Both are used to make significant pauses before the word 'this', so as to emphasize it – 'are cured. ‖ This' and 'of praise. ‖ This'. In other words, allowing for these three variations, Williams's basic unit here is without a caesura. Another way of putting that is to say that each of the three units into which the lines are divided is normally an unbroken unit in sense and breath. The lines are peculiarly broken up, not by caesuras as such, but by the way they are printed on the page. **What do you make of this way of arranging the lines? How would you describe the shape of the lines?**

DISCUSSION

Each sequence follows a similar pattern. We could either call that pattern a sequence of three short lines, stepped down the page, the majority of those lines constructed as a single rhythmic step. Or you could see each sequence of three units as a single line, divided into three rhythmic steps and aligned on the page so as to emphasize those steps and, indeed, to give weight to the pauses between them. The reading is deliberately slowed. Williams called this his 'triadic foot'. In a way, what Williams does here is to cast the traditional verse pattern, where two half-lines divide on a caesura, into a line divided into three parts with two caesuras. The effect is both visual and aural. Visually the line rocks or pivots on its central portion. Aurally the long line is hesitant, breathing, pausing, letting go. In fact the models for it are physical. The line walks, rocks, pivots and breathes. Williams described his endeavour, asserting its newness, as 'a reply to Greek and Latin with the bare hands'.[9] For him, Americans were 'loose, disassociated (linguistically), yawping speakers of a new language' who 'are privileged ... to sense and so to seek to discover that possible thing which is disturbing the metrical table of values'.[10] This is how important Williams perceived the invention of his metre, or indeed any rhythmic pattern. 'Measure' is an old word for metrical rhythm. Williams declared, 'Reluctant, we waken from our dreams. And what is reality? How do we know reality? The only reality that we can know is MEASURE.'[11] His particular measure and the thinking that informs it are immensely important for the structures that much modern poetry has adopted.

In Europe in the First World War, Wilfred Owen confronted another aspect of our modern reality, in the trenches on the Western Front. Part of his response was in verse like this, the opening of his 'Strange Meeting':

> It seemed that out of battle I escaped
> Down some profound dull tunnel, long since scooped
> Through granites which titanic wars had groined.
> Yet also there encumbered sleepers groaned,
> Too fast in thought or death to be bestirred.
> Then, as I probed them, one sprang up, and stared
> With piteous recognition in fixed eyes,
> Lifting distressful hands as if to bless.
> And by his smile, I knew that sullen hall,
> By his dead smile I knew we stood in Hell.[12]

You will, by now, see readily that this is fairly straightforward iambic pentameter. And you should also respond to the vowel- and consonant-music in 'some profound dull tunnel', 'granites which titanic', 'encumbered sleepers' and 'sullen hall' – all careful uses of quantity to add sonority, gloom or sharpness to the lines. **But what do you make of the rhymes?**

DISCUSSION

This kind of rhyme ('groined'/'groaned') is called pararhyme. Obviously we could speak of these rhymes in much the same way as we have been commenting on all the uses of sound-pattern in previous examples, as means of fusing the words of the poem together, of shaping it. But clearly something additional is happening here. The couplet form leads us to expect full rhymes – after all, that's what we usually get – but we don't get them. Instead, we get a sequence of dislocated expectations, jarring poetic shocks. It's not that the sounds of the rhymes themselves are inherently upsetting but rather that, instead of the resolution a rhyme effects, we get a disturbance. We don't have to say, in other words, that 'scooped', for example, is a word we find emotionally disturbing, but only that our structures of expectation have been disturbed.

That series of shocks, generated through poetic structures, both parallels and assists the larger shock that 'Strange Meeting' as a whole generates. In turn, we have to say that it is a response, a literary echo, of the shock of the trenches. We are not concerned with the bare study of poetic device. The devices fit into contexts of palpable, not merely patterned, meanings. 'Literature', wrote Ezra Pound, 'does not exist in a vacuum.'[13] Nor do the structures at its heart. These propositions will be central to the next two chapters.

5. Why Patterns Change: the Fourteenth and Sixteenth Centuries

No poetic structure exists in a vacuum. This is the proposition I would like to test now. If poetic structures do not exist in vacuums, then studying them takes on a depth of meaning well beyond the technical assessment of a rhythm or the recognition of a rhyme-scheme. We can argue against any idea of 'pure' poetry, somehow above the battle, an abstracted essence. We will look at examples from times when the condition of poetry in England was changing radically and ask whether that change shadowed a wider cultural change. In this chapter we will consider examples from the fourteenth century and the sixteenth century. It's not the usual meaning for the word, but I will call this an exercise in 'sociometrics'.[1]

Here is a passage from a fourteenth-century Middle English romance, *Sir Orfeo*.[2] It's a version of the Orpheus story. Orfeo, in order to recover his wife, who has been snatched into the

Underworld, follows her disguised as a minstrel. The language may look a bit strange, but read it aloud, trying to make it flow, even swing. As to the poem's structure, what seem to be its main features? Look at rhyme, syllable and stress. You may find it hard to be precise about syllables. Don't worry: get as close as you can – there are plenty of uncertainties about medieval language-values. Most important, does the poem seem to you a poem to be heard or one to be read? How would a fourteenth-century audience have experienced it, do you think? Here, then, Orfeo has entered the Underworld. (The more unfamiliar words are glossed in note 3 to this chapter.)

> When he was in the roche y-go,
> Wele three mile other mo,
> He com into a fair cuntray,
> As bright so sonne on somers day,
> Smothe and plain and all grene,
> Hille no dale was ther non y-sene.
> Amidde the lond a castel he sighe,
> Riche and real and wonder heighe.
> All the utmast wall
> Was clere and shine as cristal.
> An hundred tours ther were about
> Degiselich and bataild stout.
> The butras com out of the diche,
> Of rede gold y-arched riche.
> The vousour was avowed all
> Of ich maner divers aumal
> Within ther wer wide wones
> All of precious stones.
> The werst piler on to biholde
> Was all of burnist gold.[3]

DISCUSSION

I said that Orfeo disguises himself as a minstrel, and it's probable that this is the sort of story a minstrel might have told in a marketplace or a nobleman's hall. It would be a performance. But even if *Sir Orfeo* is a poem that would normally be performed, this version has been written down – otherwise we wouldn't have it now. It may have been written down from a performance or as a sort of script to be remembered or as a literary 'refinement' of an oral story. But the probability is that oral performance preceded written text. I have already used the word 'version' to describe *Sir Orfeo*, and one way of sensing the 'oral' manner of the poem is to compare it with other manuscript versions which have survived. Here is another version of some of the lines:

When he had therin go
A myle or els-two,
He com into a feyre cuntrey
Als bryght as son in somerys dey:
Hyll ne dale was ther non sen;
It was a welle feyre gren.
Orfeo full wele it seye,
A feyre castel, ryall and hyghe.[4]

The existence of various versions is itself evidence of various prior performances. This one represents another way the story might have been heard. You will notice the many differences. But certainly if we heard either version we would say we had been listening to *Sir Orfeo*. The situation is like two comedians telling versions of the same joke. The comedians will be full of nuance, embellishments, ad libs. Afterwards the joke will be the same, but the performances will be remembered as different. Of the Spanish *romance*, a form comparable with the English medieval romance, the Spanish scholar Menéndez Pidal said that it existed in its variants. That is to say, we can only identify what the poem is in the whole range of its performances, where it may truly be said to exist, and not as it is stabilized on the page. With *Sir Orfeo*, and poems like it, we are witnessing a crucial shift from oral performance to the stability of script. And implied in that will be a shift from communal audience to private reader, not yet fully grown but, at least, waiting to be born.

To get back to the initial analysis I asked you to do, how far does your account of the structures provide evidence for the oral nature of the lines? You should also involve the lines from the second version, which I introduced to make clear the central fact of oral poetry, that it is a poetry of performance.

DISCUSSION

I would look first to the rhythm – mainly three or four heavy stresses to the line and so, overall, approximating to an eight-syllabled line. This is combined with a couplet rhyme using easy-to-remember rhymes. It's not precisely the octosyllabic couplet we have here: it's in no way as stabilized as that. But, again, we can say that the later, written, story-telling form is waiting to be born. I say 'story-telling' form because lines that short, with swiftly arriving rhymes, encourage the performer not to digress nor to indulge description but to get on with it. The audience wants to know what happens. Characteristically in these stories, emotions are clear and understandable, stereotyped, if you like. Description is unadorned, except in set-pieces like a description of a castle. Such set-pieces may well be interchangeable between stories: 'How do you do your castles?' is the sort of question one performer might ask another. And notice just such a handy performing device in the shortcut description 'The werst piler on to biholde / Was all of burnist gold', describing all the pillars by describing one only, the worst, which is everybody else's best.

Notice how, between the two versions, the rhymes are almost identical, stable in a pattern of little variations. Did these performers, I wonder, concentrate on recalling a set of rhymes as well as a story – certain points of arrival within the narrative texture? The mnemonic power of rhyme is undoubtedly important in oral performance. The rhymes, too, are straightforward, not placing too much strain on the performer's memory or imagination or the learning of the audience. But, remember, an oral society has its own modes of knowledge and enhanced powers of memory, often well in excess of our memories, depleted by our capacity to store and locate information, and so not feel the need to remember it.

Finally, between the two versions of these lines from *Sir Orfeo*, the metrical drive is the same, though, in matters of detail, there is considerable variation. The day has not yet come when a poet – Oscar Wilde – will say he's done a hard day's work – 'I spent all morning putting a comma in and all afternoon taking it out.' Clearly, in *Sir Orfeo* a different conception of what constitutes a poem is at work from what would operate today. The oral poem is more to be understood through its basic drive and content than in the fixity and inalienability of its detail. It fits into a social condition where most people will not have recourse to script but will rely on their delight in performance and the considerable powers of the performing memory.

Now look at the following piece, from one of the greatest poems in the English language, William Langland's *Piers Plowman*.[5] It is a long religious poem, told in a series of dreams and visions. These lines begin Langland's visionary account of Christ's passion. The dreamer goes to sleep and sees Christ as he enters Jerusalem. **Again, in pursuit of the verse's structures, look for rhymes, count syllables, look at the distribution of heavy (and therefore light) stresses, and see (this is most important with Langland and a number of other medieval poets) whether there are any other elements which seem to give structure to the lines. Look at the beginnings of words. I keep saying 'look', but really I mean read the words aloud and, in that way, look. (Difficult words are glossed in note 6.)**

Wolleward and watschod wente I forth aftur
As a recheles renke that recheth nat of sorwe,
And yede forth ylike a lorel al my lyf-tyme,
Til I waxe wery of the world and wilnede efte to slepe
And lened me to lenten and long tyme I slepte.
Of gurles and of *gloria laus* greetliche me dremede
And how *osanna* by orgene olde folke songe.
One semblable to the Samaritan and somdeel to Peres the Plouhman,
Barfot on an asse back botles cam prikynge.[6]

DISCUSSION

Let's see what doesn't work first. Is there a regular syllable-count?
No. And there's no rhyme. There's nothing like an iambic beat
here, or even the looser but clear beat that there was in the
extracts from *Sir Orfeo*. Yet there is an unmistakable pulse that
drives the voice on. Indeed, there are quite a lot of passages in
Piers Plowman – this is not one of them – where the poem seems
rather like a boxer sparring for an opening, not doing very much,
and only this beat, like the boxer's rhythmic limb and body
movements, seems to sustain it. The beat largely coincides, in each
line, with words that begin with the same letter – alliterate – four
beats to the line, with three alliterating.

When we use alliteration, we use words which have the
same initial sound close enough together for us to notice. The
words form an aural pattern which has a similar effect to rhyme,
drawing the elements of each line together; and, as each line is
tightened, so, in turn, is the whole verse structure. In modern
poetry, alliteration is used as an occasional device in a com-
paratively unsystematic way, as a special effect, if you like. But
Langland's poem is constructed around the device, as were a large
number of major fourteenth-century poems. Together, these
poems constitute the fourteenth-century alliterative revival. They
were written mainly in the North and the Midlands. Langland
himself was from the West Midlands. The style is generally held to
relate in some way to the patterns of Old English verse (hence
'revival'), which was also strongly stressed and alliterative, though
characteristically using a shorter line. Langland's line has typically
a lot of light stresses, and is capable of sustaining them. The
combined weight of heavy stress and alliteration, thudding down
on the words, ensures that there is no loss of control even in the
longest lines. If we use the word 'rhyme' very broadly, then alliteration increases massively the rhyme-like cohesion of the lines.

One other feature of Old English verse was that its lines were
constructed out of two half-lines divided, much like T. S. Eliot's

lines by a heavy caesura. **Does it seem to you that Langland's lines might also respond to such a division?**

DISCUSSION

Well, some of them could easily be read like that:

Wolleward and watschod ‖ wente I forth aftur
As a recheles renke ‖ that recheth nat of sorwe,
And yede forth ylike a lorel ‖ al my lyf-tyme,

and, strongest of all:

Barfot on an asse back ‖ botles cam prikynge.

These half-lines correspond to a spoken phrasing, the first half-line carrying the alliterative weight (two alliterating stresses). This is echoed in the second half-line (one alliterating stress) and subtly modulated by association with another heavy stress but this time less pointed, because not alliterating. It's often the case that the first half-line ends on a heavy stress and so, taken overall, is rising in the way we speak it. And the second half-line often ends in a light stress and so, taken overall, is falling in the way we speak it. It may well be that the reduced number of alliterative stresses in the second half-line assists this sense of fall. So, counterpointing with the driving alliterative rhythm is a rhythm of rise and fall, fully integrated with the structures of sound and stress. The rise is up to the half-line division and the fall down from it. A lot of power is concentrated within Langland's line and yet each line has its own tension released to begin again, wave-like, with the next line and its fresh alliteration.

The socio-metric point here is that Langland and the alliteratists were regional, not London-oriented, in their methods. The alliterative revival may have shadowed a division which is still perpetuated; a differential concern between London, the seat of power, and the country's varied regions, indeed, its varied nations. The structural point – less exciting but, to me at least, still rewarding to note – is that in Langland we have another major poet writing in English whose verse, like T. S. Eliot's six hundred years later, falls well outside the iambic pattern but is nonetheless strongly rhythmic.

At this point, we must look at the court poet Geoffrey Chaucer. So far, of the many fourteenth-century possibilities, we have examined two metrical modes: narrative couplets, approximating very roughly to the octosyllabic, and Langland's alliterative line. With Chaucer, and in the context of metre, the main question we have to ask is: what kind of line is he writing? In particular, is it iambic? In the light of the foregoing discussion of Langland's versification, and especially the sense of rise to and fall from the half-line break, read aloud the following lines from Chaucer's *The Pardoner's Tale*. The reading break, called the *virga* (indicated thus /) and present in some manuscript versions of Chaucer, is retained. I should say again, as I did at the beginning of this chapter, that medieval language values are often contentious. In the case of Chaucer's metre, the degree to which the final *e* on words was or was not given sound, indeed syllabic, value in poetry ('peyne'/'pleyne') is disputed. Obviously this would affect questions of metre. My feeling is that Chaucer sounded it when he wanted to and didn't when he didn't. It was, in other words, an option for him. The more it is used, the smoother, the more lingering, the rhythm. And my guess is that sometimes Chaucer wanted the rhythm smooth and sometimes he didn't. For instance, in this line from *The Pardoner's Tale*:

> As riot / hasard / stewes / and tavernes

I would like to scan 'stewès' but would not be fussed about whether I read 'tavernès' or 'tavernes'. In practice I would tend to linger a little on the '-es', letting the sound echo into the end-line pause. I suppose, in fact, that is the basis of my sense of the final *e* generally; that it was by this time – the fourteenth century – more an echo than fully syllabic, unless for a particular effect the poet wanted it to be so. In any case, the passage I've chosen isn't much affected rhythmically by final *es*. It is about Adam in Paradise.

> He was in Paradys / and whan that he
> Eet of the frut / defended on a tree
> Anon he was out cast / to wo and peyne
> O glotonye / on thee wel oghte us pleyne[7]

What kind of metre have you got here? Or a better way of putting that is: how can you read the lines?

DISCUSSION

Well, it looks like iambic pentameter. As compared with both *Sir Orfeo*, which is only loosely octosyllabic, and *Piers Plowman*, which takes no notice of syllable-count, Chaucer is concerned to write ten-syllabled lines here, presumably on Continental – French or Italian – models. That it is, in fact, iambic is more problematic. It's hard to see these lines as each carrying more than four heavy stresses, and it might be worth calling it an accentual four-stress line. But this seems to me a 'wraparound' term which doesn't at all attempt to describe the alternating current behind the lines. That alternating current is precisely what we call iambic. It may be that the line is lighter (that is, carrying less than the expected five stresses) in order to promote the speed that seems appropriate to oral story-telling. *The Pardoner's Tale* would have been read aloud to an audience just as *Sir Orfeo* was. Its probable audience would be courtly rather than popular, but remember that the dramatic setting of *The Canterbury Tales*, from which *The Pardoner's Tale* comes, is of a group of people from a wide spread of social classes on the road, on pilgrimage.

The *virga*, though, at least suggests the possibility that the lines could be read with a rise and fall within the line. If we observe the pauses as we read, the iambic impression recedes, though it doesn't disappear. The *virga* seems to shape the verse, not as metre only, but as thought and speech, and to indicate the counterpointed rhythm which operates within the metrical sequence. It may be that this rising and falling rhythm is related to the way Latin chant was sung in church, using rising and falling sequences called 'cadences'. Ian Robinson, in his book *Chaucer's Prosody*, offers an excellent description of Chaucer's line which resolves these possibilities. He calls it 'balanced pentameter' and so allows for a metre which works as well in the half-line as it does in analysis by feet.[8]

The fourteenth century was a period of immense metrical variety. We have looked at three poems from that range: a manuscript account of an oral romance, a large-scale alliterative religious work in a West Midlands dialect and a poem by Chaucer – a presence at the court of Richard II – in a metre which, after some vicissitudes and a resurrection in the sixteenth century, was to dominate English verse till the 1900s. I am hoping to construct some sense of how structural change in poetry might shadow change in society. **From these metrical examples, can you glean some hints as to how this might be possible?**

DISCUSSION

I ask the question so tentatively partly because it is in itself difficult and partly to forestall you saying, as Bertrand Russell is reported to have said to God when he arrived in heaven, 'You didn't give us enough evidence.' We can only proceed by hints here, but let us proceed.

First, we seem, in the fourteenth century to be in a period when poetry is given and received as oral performance and bears many of the marks of such performance. This is clearest in *Sir Orfeo*, but is apparent even in the lines from the court-centred Chaucer. It would require a great deal more evidence and evaluation for us to assert that the fourteenth century was a period in which oral and literate transmission, memory and reading, improvisation and text are in a state of some flux as to what is to be prime, but that is the way the hints would be tending. And the very stability and capacity for invariance that written transmission promises will affect not only the art of the word but also the way we perceive the world and our relation to it.

Second, the strongly regional manner of *Piers Plowman* suggests some degree of assertion within the English regions, based on a traditional 'English' view of writing as distinct from the newfangled modes of London and the court based on Continental, particularly French, models. The fact that the alliterative metres disappear and that the iambic survives may echo a general process of centralization. In such an account, the alliterative metres are a last-ditch flourish drawing on the indigenous reserves of the English accentual tradition. Indeed the whole battle between syllable-count and stress-count can be read as echoing contending views of the nation and its political and class structures, where alliteration and stress become indicators of Englishness and pre-capitalism, and the iambic foot and syllable-counting indicate French and bourgeois supplanting. I say 'can be', not 'should be': I don't quite believe this. But clearly something is going on. And one of the things that is going on is fairly wholesale French influence on English society and indeed its naturalization.[9] I spoke earlier of *Piers Plowman* as being 'one of the greatest poems in the English language'. I could have added that it is the greatest unread poem in the language. That eclipse may never have been impartial. More manuscripts of *Piers Plowman* survive than of any other poem of its day. Why should it be so little read even now? Did Langland's metre struggle, triumph and die for political imperatives?

If I now jump from the fourteenth to the sixteenth century, this is not because nothing happened in between. Far from it. Rather it is because the poetry of Sir Thomas Wyatt, the poet I want us to look at next, seems in some ways to be wrestling with the metrical questions implied by Chaucer's practice.

The sixteenth century, like the fourteenth, was a period of immense change and invention in poetry. Much of it was stimulated by the invention of printing. So the jump to the sixteenth century enables us to chart the next stage in the change, from oral production to script and now to print. The stability and wide multiple distribution of 'the text' has massive consequences, some of which we will be able at least to glimpse in the rest of this chapter. We will be mainly looking at sonnets, but first look at these two versions of the opening lines of a celebrated poem, though not a sonnet, by Sir Thomas Wyatt. The first is a manuscript version from the most important of the Wyatt manuscripts, the Egerton manuscript in the British Library. The second is the first printed version, in Richard Tottel's 'miscellany' *Songes and Sonettes*, published in 1557, fifteen years after Wyatt's death. The Egerton text is:

> They fle from me that sometyme did me seke
> With naked fote stalking in my chambre.
> I have sene theim gentill tame and meke
> That nowe are wyld and do not remembre
> That sometyme they put theimself in daunger
> To take bred at my hand; and nowe they raunge
> Besely seking with a continuell chaunge.[10]

And the Tottel:

> They flee from me, that somtime did me seke
> With naked fote stalkyng within my chamber.
> Once have I seen them gentle, tame, and meke,
> That now are wild, and do not once remember
> That sometyme they have put them selves in danger,
> To take bread at my hand, and now they range,
> Busily sekyng in continuall change.[11]

Can you spot the differences between these two versions? What is their effect on the distribution of stresses and on the syllable-count?

DISCUSSION

Making things regular seems to be the Tottel intention. Adding 'once' to line 3 makes the line ten syllables, and the reversal 'have I' is then required to maintain the iambic. He has allowed himself eleven syllables in all the lines with feminine endings ('chamber', 'remember', 'danger'). This may at first sight seem strange, but it is, in fact, a frequent variation in iambic pentameter. All the other changes of stress – 'within' for 'in' (line 2); adding 'once' (line 4) and 'have' (line 5); changing 'with a' to 'in' (line 7) – have the effect of clarifying or at least not harming the basic iambic drive in the poem. The only other verbal change – 'them selves' for 'theimself' in line 5 – regularizes the grammar. **The question now is: which version is to be preferred?**

DISCUSSION

There's no absolute answer to that. Obviously the Tottel editor thought that clarifying the poem as iambic was improving it. And the tendency until well into the twentieth century was to see Wyatt as an incompetent metrist, needing improvement. But then, as twentieth-century metres changed, so the subtly anguished 'irregular' line

That nowe are wyld and do not remembre

as against the too bouncy but regular

That now are wild, and do not once remember

began to be first appreciated and then understood for what it was.

One of the best lines for appreciating the power of Wyatt's effects is not in the stanza I have printed, but opens his third stanza. The Egerton manuscript has

It was no dreme: I lay brode waking.

The Tottel version is

It was no dreme: for I lay broade awakyng.

Tottel goes for smoothness of a sort: by introducing two lightly stressed syllables into the second half-line, the reader is forced to re-weight the line and the three possible heavy stresses of Egerton are prised apart. 'I lay brode waking' becomes 'for I lay broade awakyng'. 'Awakyng' may smooth the roughened stress, but it destroys the force of the total realization, in Egerton, that the forsaken lover is not dreaming but unmistakably awake.

There are similar emasculations. 'Within' in line 2, for instance. Presumably the Tottel editor wanted to separate '-ing in', but, in doing that, he loses the dramatic – I would say poignant – pause that Egerton has. You can't avoid it, as you read 'stalking in my chambre'. Another little tune has been eliminated for the sake of regularity, in changing 'with a continuell chaunge' to 'in continuall change'. Neither version is metrically bad, but what Tottel is losing or not responding to is the Wyatt 'voice'. And that voice is all over the poem. Without complete redrafting, even the Tottel approach can't smooth out 'To take bred at my hand' or 'Besely seking'. And half a voice keeps the poem in business.

In fact Wyatt's particular phrasing – what I've been calling his 'voice' – is clearest in the way he treats half-line phrases. The units in the line that disturb the iambic course are nearly all half-lines: 'Besely seking / with a continuell chaunge' is clearest, but the whole stanza can be perceived in the same way. What is lingering in Wyatt, giving him his special sound, is the music of the half-line. It is at play just as much as it had been in Chaucer. And it is this that the Tottel editor does not respond to and seeks to eliminate. Wyatt seems to be recognizing for his own style the same three elements that Ian Robinson has suggested as being present in Chaucer: iambic pentameter, the half-line division and a speech rhythm playing with the sonic space that these two differing patterns of rise and fall permit. The overall sound of the line is different but the algebra of it is kindred. I say this because Wyatt has in the past often been talked about as if he didn't know what he was doing; as if he was trying to write iambic and not quite getting there. But if he didn't know what he was doing when he wrote lines like the ones quoted from the Egerton manuscript (and they are typical) then we could all do with more of his ignorance.

I have emphasized the element of 'voice', the rhythms of speech in Wyatt, and this should serve to remind us of the oral nature of poetry. This persists even now. Even if we read privately from a printed book, poetry expects the speaking voice. The modern compromise is the speaking imagination. But speech is implied. And speech implies audience. Clearly the audience for Wyatt's lines is not the same sort of audience as the audience was for *Sir Orfeo*. There is a savouring dissection of the lover's grief in Wyatt. In the swift medieval story we witness exemplary grief and its solution through Orfeo's courage and ingenuity in winning back his wife: there is no time to dwell on the mental ramifications in our responses to the things that happen to us as, for example, seems to be the power behind Wyatt's image of his betrayers: that they had been willing to take bread at his hand. The question 'What audience?' is clearly an aspect of sociometrics, though not one I intend to enter on more deeply than to suggest that there is an intimacy of address in Wyatt, some of it at least to be gauged from the way he combines the metrical elements we have isolated. Whether the atmosphere Wyatt creates is a response to his personal griefs – in the modern term, 'confessional' – or to the conditions of close intrigue in the Tudor court or a stylized social game-playing are all questions that are worth asking and I happily present them to you, not expecting any answers just now either from you or from me.

My socio-metric point, though, is almost a technological one and it is to do with the changing relationship of poet to audience that printing brought with it. The change between Egerton and Tottel may have something to do with the reduction of the individual 'voice' known to an intimate group in favour of a 'style' which is blander and more accommodated to a wider, less accountable audience simply because it is a less individualized way of writing. The change is, in fact, quite complex. It is not so much an immediate transformation at a given historical moment as a question of an emerging tendency. Where previously the poet's words were, as it were, fleshed out, by performance directly perceived, or by audience and poet sharing the same circle, now the poet's words come disembodied, on a page, widely available as words, which our imaginations give flesh to. The poet becomes a text which we reinvent and shape ourselves. We can gauge something of the difference when we read a Shakespeare play, sitting in an armchair at home, and when we see actors perform it, *being* Antony, *being* Cleopatra. What of loss and gain there is in this is not easily registered, but, that it is different, is clear. In the particular example we have been engaged with – the difference between the Egerton manuscript and the Tottel printing – we can trace the change in a question of poetic structuring, which constitutes, if it does not fully contain that change.

Now to the sonnets. The sonnet was one of the most important forms in this experimental age. It is a fourteen-line poem, its form, originally developed in Italy and associated with Francesco Petrarch (1304–74). It was much imitated in England, initially by Wyatt and the Earl of Surrey and later by Sir Philip Sidney. Here is a sonnet by Sidney. **First of all, how does its metre compare with the lines from either of the versions of Wyatt's poem?**

> Leave me o Love, which reachest but to dust,
> And thou my mind aspire to higher things:
> Grow rich in that which never taketh rust:
> What ever fades, but fading pleasure brings.
>
> Draw in thy beames, and humble all thy might
> To that sweet yoke, where lasting freedomes be:
> Which breakes the clowdes and opens forth the light,
> That doth both shine and give us sight to see.
>
> O take fast hold, let that light be thy guide
> In this small course which birth draws out to death,
> And thinke how evill becommeth him to slide,
> Who seeketh heav'n, and comes of heav'nly breath.
>   Then farewell world, thy uttermost I see,
>   Eternall Love maintaine thy life in me.[12]

DISCUSSION

Well, it has a much smoother flow. That flow is a fairly settled unambiguous iambic. There is no need to read the metre by the half-line. The iambic flow controls the line. Even the initial trochees – 'Leave me', 'Grow rich', 'Draw in' – allow something very close to iambic stress. The only line which might seem to disrupt the smooth finish is 'And thinke how evill becommeth him to slide', where there is an extra light syllable, 'be-'. This is a mild irregularity, but it could have been made slightly more regular if Sidney had dropped the initial 'And', so starting with a pair of trochees. Or he could have made the iambic stress as well as the syllable-count regular by writing 'And thinke how evill causeth him to slide' or 'And thinke how sin becommeth him to slide'. All this would be in pursuit of the regularity which seems to be what Sidney had in mind. With another voice, like Wyatt's, the line as Sidney first had it would cause no problem. It is all a matter of exploiting the limitations and the benefits of our characteristic style, of playing to our strengths. And so it may be that Sidney here deliberately breaks the pattern he has been so careful to set up. The slight metrical hitch may be intended to echo the hitch in life that the urgings of evil also bring. Maybe.

The construct that Sidney has achieved here is, in itself, a compendium of the possibilities of the iambic pentameter. A line like 'What ever fades, but fading pleasure brings' opens up eighteenth-century vistas, and countless hymns are possible with 'Eternall Love maintaine thy life in me' behind them. Sidney represents and gathers together, so that they can be launched upon succeeding generations, the implications of Chaucerian iambic. Only the unreconstructed 'And thinke how evill becommeth him to slide' carries with it other, medieval, rhythmical implications – those maintained by Wyatt. Although there is something wistful and injured about Wyatt's metrical voice, its particular broken rhythms seem to me if not to imply then to allow John Donne, full of vigorous uncertainty, more directly than does Sidney's all-confident iambic sweep. Here is a Donne sonnet.

If poisonous minerals, and if that tree,
Whose fruit threw death on else immortal us,
If lecherous goats, if serpents envious
Cannot be damn'd; alas! why should I be?
Why should intent or reason, born in me,
Make sins, else equal, in me more heinous?
And mercy being easy, and glorious

To God; in His stern wrath, why threatens He?
But who am I, that dare dispute with Thee
O God? Oh! of thine only worthy blood,
And my tears, make a heavenly Lethean flood,
And drown in it my sin's black memory;
That Thou remember them, some claim as debt,
I think it mercy, if Thou wilt forget.[13]

I'll pause only to point out the line 'Whose fruit threw death on else immortal us' for its bold emphases, which test the limits of iambic and draw out the intellectual possibilities of a poem that can put legitimate, and not merely metrical, heavy stress on words like 'else' and 'us'.

Now could you look closely at the rhyme-schemes of the sonnets by Sidney and Donne? Tabulate them, and see how far that straightforward act helps you describe the way each poem works. Initially concentrate on the Sidney; after that the Donne. Look particularly at the eighth line in the Donne. What position does it occupy in the way the poem develops its thought? This whole investigation is based on the idea that particular arrangements of rhyme (rhyme-schemes) suit particular structures of thought. It may not be just that they suit the structures of thought. We must be alert to the possibility that they specify or enforce these thoughts. If I say 'clickety-click' there's a chance you may say '66'. People of a certain age and whimsy (and a feeling for accuracy) will say, 'See you later, alligator' and hope for the reply, '*After* a while, crocodile.' Rhyme may produce prescribed responses. Negatively, we saw at the end of the last chapter how Owen's rhymes were used deliberately to frustrate expectations. A pattern of rhymes – a scheme – simply extends these possibilities for shaping our responses beyond the meanings of individual words to the recurrent forms that contain and control them. The sonnet is one of Europe's stock shapes, tight and demanding and putting down a pattern on thought. Ezra Pound once spent a whole year writing a sonnet a day to keep himself in trim.[14] Now, back to Sidney and Donne.

DISCUSSION

The rhyme-schemes are, at one and the same time, simple and intricate: simple, in that they are based on very few rhymes; intricate, in that those few rhymes interlock the poems quatrain by quatrain, by means of the sonic patterns they set up, and then they allow the final couplet to stand out as conclusion.

Sidney's use of the sonnet scheme is the less strenuous of the two and, in that sense, the less coercive and more 'natural'. It guides the poem gently, holding it together while not pushing itself forward as brilliant in itself – ABAB CDCD EFEF DD. This is the 'English' form of the sonnet, ending with a couplet. The 'Italian' form (used equally by English poets) divides the poem into its first eight lines – the octave – and then its last six lines – the sestet. The octave rhymes ABBA ABBA, and the sestet can rhyme over two or three new rhymes, but interlocked, not usually ending in a couplet. In practice there are all sorts of hybrids and ingenuities. To be simple about it, an Italian sonnet divides its lines 8 + 6 and an English sonnet divides them 4 + 4 + 4 (= 12) + 2. The English sonnet always ends on a couplet. But many English sonnets superimpose an octave/sestet pattern (8 + 6) on the 12 + 2 pattern. We could numerically represent the way that comes out as (4 + 4) + (4 + 2).

A sonnet is divided in two senses complementary to each other: by interlocking rhymes and by the way the argument develops. The sonnet will thus often present an excellent example of the way a form and a rhyme-scheme can assist, even insist on, a particular type of logical movement. For example, in the Donne sonnet, even though an English type, the argument in the octave proceeds 'if . . . if . . . why . . . why?'; the sestet continues with a 'but . . .' quatrain and concludes with a couplet, a conclusion which is also a plea to God. In the octave, Donne has used arguments of 'reason' and reason only, not addressing God directly but saying, 'why threatens He?' God is the subject of an address to us, the reader, or of a self-address, by Donne to Donne. In the third quatrain, Donne addresses God directly – 'O God?' – and deprecates himself. And in the final couplet he throws himself upon the hope of God's mercy. In this case, the couplet, by formally introducing an entirely new rhyme (but notice that it brings the rhymes used in the fourteen lines to only four, which is pretty tight), enforces the modulation of thought, almost release, that this strenuous sonnet finally achieves. Without that new rhyme marking out the full conclusion, the final sestet might be seen as a continuous and undifferentiated prayer ('make . . . drown . . . forget'). Instead the couplet marks a real modulation, from a prayer of request to a prayer of abandonment to divine mercy. Donne is no longer calling the shots. Again, the octave and the sestet have their point of change indicated by the introduction of a new rhyme (the third) in the third quatrain. Up to this point only two had been used: ABBA ABBA ACCA DD.

I haven't mentioned syllables yet, except initially in the case of the Sidney sonnet. Usually sonnets are written in pentameter but as with most poetic forms, a liberty well taken is its own justification. I want you to read a third sonnet now, by the twentieth-century poet Charles Causley. Part of my intention here is to show how a modern post-Eliot poet can still use and develop a traditional form. **I want you to look first at the number of syllables in Causley's lines and also to tabulate the rhyme-scheme. What in each case do you notice? Meanwhile keep thinking about Donne's eighth line. I haven't forgotten about it.** Now here is Charles Causley's sonnet:

> I am the great sun, but you do not see me,
>   I am your husband, but you turn away.
> I am the captive, but you do not free me,
>   I am the captain you will not obey.
>
> I am the truth, but you will not believe me,
>   I am the city where you will not stay,
> I am your wife, your child, but you will leave me,
>   I am that God to whom you will not pray.
>
> I am your counsel, but you do not hear me,
>   I am the lover whom you will betray,
> I am the victor, but you do not cheer me,
>   I am the holy dove whom you will slay.
>
> I am your life, but if you will not name me,
> Seal up your soul with tears, and never blame me.[15]

DISCUSSION

In the matter of syllables, there is a particular ingenuity here, which is an ingenuity of meaning too. Every other line has eleven syllables. There is an extra-metrical syllable therefore: 'me'. But the 'me' of the poem is also the entirely metrical 'I': 'I am the great sun, but you do not see | me' (10 + 1). The I/me personage is then both the source of the poem, by the fact of speaking it, and outside it, not acknowledged and taken up by 'you' – the person addressed, who is maybe the poet, the reader or humanity in general, or all of them together. This 'outsider' quality is indicated by the extra-metricality of its name: 'me'. This 11/10 syllable alternation is obviously a variation, and an unusual one, for a sonnet, as also is the fact that Causley uses only two rhymes throughout: ABAB ABAB ABAB AA. You might say that's easy enough with the constant 'me' throughout, alternating with one of the most fecund rhyme sounds in English – 'away'/'stay'/ 'pray'/'betray'/'slay'. Nonetheless, if you think it's easy try it sometime and, above all, try to keep it as natural as Causley does.

But now take a second look at each of the lines ending in 'me'. Look at the penultimate word in each of them. What do you notice? (You may be ahead of me. I hope you are.)

DISCUSSION

There is, indeed, another ingenuity to be contemplated here. These penultimate syllables in the 'me' lines (that is, the tenth syllables) set up a rhyme-scheme of their own – 'see'/'free'; 'believe'/'leave'; 'hear'/'cheer'; 'name'/'blame' – so that, in addition to Causley's 'extended' sonnet-scheme ABAB ABAB ABAB AA, there is concealed within it a true ten-syllabled sonnet rhyming ABAB CBCB DBDB EE. By coincidence, the 'A' rhyme of the concealed sonnet is 'see'/'free', which rhymes with the running 'A' rhyme 'me' and so rhymes with the concluding couplet in the 'extended' sonnet-pattern.

The marvel of all this is not just – or even mainly – that it's very ingenious, but that the ingenuity is combined with an extreme directness of statement. The syntax and sense are entirely unforced. Furthermore, in the 'outsiderness' of the extra-metrical 'me', we have, in effect, a metaphysical confirmation of the poem's meaning – that we exclude 'the great sun' from the meaning of our lives.

Could you now look at Causley's eighth line – that is to say, at the final line of the octave? Does it, like Donne's, indicate a climax in the development of the poem's argument?

DISCUSSION

Well yes, it does. The poem has hitherto been conducted as a riddle where we are expected to divine who the 'I' is who can, at one and the same time, be 'sun', 'husband', 'captive', 'captain', 'truth', 'city', 'wife', 'child'. In the eighth line, the 'riddle' is answered – the 'I' comes out into the open: 'I am that God to whom you will not pray.' We should, though, notice that even here, the riddling tone is still preserved, in the word 'that'. Who is this God – which one? That question is matched by the pun – or is it? – in 'sun' (Son) and the allusion to the Christian Holy Spirit – or is it? – in 'holy dove'. The concealed meanings in all this are metaphysical statements paralleling the hidden rhymes and, indeed, the whole structure of the poem.[16]

The climax, then, that we might almost expect at the end of the poem, arrives at the end of the octave, just where the sonnet form suggests it should; but it is, again paralleling the overall meaning and rhythm of the poem, a negative conclusion – 'to whom you will not pray' – much as Donne arrived at the bleak 'why threatens He?' in exactly the same line of his sonnet: the eighth line, the end of the octave. At this point Donne turns the poem round by switching the direction of the poem's address – 'But who am I, that dare dispute with Thee / O God?' Causley's 'I' does no such thing but, having come out into the open, continues remorselessly on, piling up the riddling terms – 'counsel', 'lover', 'victor', 'holy dove' – until reaching the poem's second climax, in the concluding couplet, where 'your life' becomes the overall summation of all we have been rejecting throughout the poem, simply by not naming it.

The only chink of light in this process is the climactic word (in a stressed position) 'if'. 'If' the name is uttered then the massed negatives would deconstruct. Indeed, if we can address ourselves to one last structural effect in the poem, the only possibility for that reversal is already given in the poem, in every first half-line, except in the poem's conclusion – 'I am the great sun...', 'I am...' and so on. The poem's celebration, is, in fact, implicit in the range and succession of these positive attributes: elemental (sun), familial (husband, wife, child), social (captive, captain, city, victor), of the spirit (counsel, lover, holy dove) and, finally, total (God, life). The recalcitrance of the negative half-lines is never petty either, but, at its strongest, speaks with its own existential dignity. In Sartre's phrase, 'man is condemned to freedom'.[17]

Notice here, that, while examining a poetically expressed argument, the elements that have allowed us to distinguish the terms of the argument are metrical and structural: hidden rhyme, the remorselessly continued rhyme 'me' and, finally, what we can reasonably call 'balanced pentameter' – a metrical pattern that served Chaucer, surfacing buoyant in a mid-twentieth-century Causley.

To conclude, I want to look back again to the time when this poetic structure, the sonnet, which is clearly still alive, first came to England: the sixteenth century. I have suggested that changes in poetic method are occasioned by social developments or else parallel them. For the fourteenth century, we looked at the narrative couplet, alliterative verse and the iambic line emergent in iambic pentameter. For the sixteenth century, we have traced some of the resources and development of iambic writing and have looked closely at the possibilities in the rhymes and structures of the sonnet, a form deriving from Italian practice. Coincident with the sonnet's arrival in England was another signal change in European possibilities: the invention of printing.

Just as we watched a medieval move from oral delivery to, at least, preservation by script, so in the sixteenth century we move from script to print.[18] Increasingly printed poetry will require *readers*, and so literacy. The medieval poet had a listening audience, mainly unlettered. If we project the wider implications of this change where information is largely transmitted through print, reading becomes vital for the accumulation of particular kinds of privileged information and a social split may open up based on book knowledge and the opportunity to acquire it. Audiences will be regarded as different with respect to the types of things that can be addressed to them. Most dangerous of all, reading skill and intelligence may be equated, a false devaluation of all types of oral knowledge, and of peoples whose skills and cultures are oral. Much of this is to be in the future, but the technological sanction for it comes to birth in the sixteenth century.

However, I want now to speak more of particulars and of the consequences to poetry of 'seeing' the poem on the page. **Here is part of a poem by George Herbert. It is admittedly an extreme example. Put it beside the Sidney or the Donne, or, even more to the point, beside the extract from *Sir Orfeo* on page 61. What is the change implicit here? The poem is called 'Easter-wings' and this is the first of two stanzas, both the same shape.**

> Lord, who createdst man in wealth and store,
>   Though foolishly he lost the same,
>   Decaying more and more,
>   Till he became
>   Most poore:
>   With thee
>   O let me rise
>   As larks, harmoniously,
>   And sing this day thy victories:
> Then shall the fall further the flight in me.[19]

DISCUSSION

Herbert's poem is, as I said, an extreme example of the new possibilities afforded by print. The poem could now take on a visual life, where its shape on the page became important, even, in this case, an emblem of the poem's meaning. The shortest lines in the stanza – the mid-lines – are at once the most reduced spiritually ('Most poore') and the point at which increase begins ('With thee').

Medieval illustration, when it was at all elaborated, had tended to be a matter of borders and frames, embellishing a lumpish (visually speaking) piece of text. It was visually complex and whole, but the wholeness was of the page, not of the poem. Capital letters got out of hand and crowded out the few words of text that were allowed into their set-pieces by the illuminators. Letter overcame text. It was a visual art with its own glories, but it was an art to embellish the text, to contribute its insights, certainly, but not, as with Herbert, to be the text itself.[20] In a Renaissance printed text, embellishments – characteristically, simple emblematic devices – become subjects for poems and, indeed, the poem's manner. Poetry itself, spurred by a process born from the requirements of woodblock printing, could employ an emblematic style like Herbert's, which had both flourish and spareness.

Two other things are conditioned by the invention of printing. One is the care that can be devoted to stabilizing the words of a poem. Whereas a poet like Langland would seem to be less concerned with the exact placing of every word than with the drive of his verse and, above all, with his meaning, print will encourage a poet or an editor to fret over punctuation, rhythmic exactitude and so on. Thus the early printing of Wyatt's poetry resulted in its being cast in an often insensitive iambic form by altering a syllable here and there – tinkering. But a poet could tinker too, because his words were now stable and could outlast mortality and change.

> Not marble, nor the gilded monuments
> Of princes, shall outlive this powerful rime;

writes (more than says) Shakespeare. And again:

> And yet to times in hope my verse shall stand,
> Praising thy worth, despite his cruel hand.[21]

Equally, many of the slightly closeted effects we have been isolating in the rhymes and structures of Donne and Sidney are more noticeable on the page than they would be in reading. We just do not hear rhymes, intricately placed, as quickly as we see them. (This may not be true, however, of a genuinely oral culture, with its greater powers of memory and oral recognition.) The stability of print will also allow us to count syllables with greater care and the poet to regulate them more exactly. When we hear a poem delivered orally, it is not invariably clear to us how many syllables there are to a line, to put it mildly; but any fool – as I have shown by example in this book – can count, more or less, the syllables in a printed line. So naturally the poet, anxious not to appear a fool as well, and wishing to be seen to get it right, will be much more wary of the way the syllables are going.

A second consequence of printing is that the audience the poet can envisage need no longer be communal but can be seen as an individual, or an aggregation of individuals, even if unknown to the poet. This will emphasize a style of writing that can appeal to an individualized audience because it proceeds from an articulate individual who personally revolves common problems of conscience and feeling. So we get the ironic situation developing among some poets, and rising to excess in the twentieth century, of private griefs paraded before an unknown, complicit public. Far from being unwilling to intrude on private grief, printing absolutely demands that we do, but in the careful distance of print. It is a thin substitute for community. This unloosing of the individual into the public place corresponds with the Reformation's print-driven espousing of the individual but vocal conscience, reading its Bible in private and proclaiming individual accounts of it to all comers. From the communal world of *Sir Orfeo* on, the audience, as it enlarges, so it fragments. This is not to state a preference for individual or community as providing the fitter audience, but to present and mirror a social change through which it was, perhaps, historically ordained that we should find out a political leader who could say that there was no such thing as society but only individuals.

In the next chapter I want to continue this type of sociometric investigation of poetic structures, looking in the main at the eighteenth and early nineteenth centuries and, in those contexts, at the rhymed couplet and blank verse.

6. Why Patterns Change: from Classical to Romantic

I want now to look at the change from a classical to a romantic
sensibility that is generally held to have taken place from the late
eighteenth to the early nineteenth century.[1] To particularize our
initial discussion, I want to examine various handlings of the
rhyming couplet, the poetic form that is so very characteristic of
much of the best writing in the eighteenth century. I would like,
though, to start chronologically earlier than the eighteenth century, not in any attempt to plug historical gaps, but, more to the
point in the context of this book, to see what it is possible to do
with rhyming couplets. So far we've looked at *Sir Orfeo*. For
another way to use them, then, read these lines from the seven-
teenth-century satirical poem *Hudibras*, by Samuel Butler. Here is
part of a description of Hudibras's command of language. **What
effect does the use of couplets have on Butler's jokes?**

> For rhetoric, he could not ope
> His mouth, but out there flew a trope;
> And when he happened to break off
> I' th' middle of his speech, or cough,
> H' had hard words, ready to show why,
> And tell what rules he did it by;
> Else when with greatest art he spoke,
> You'd think he talked like other folk.
> For all a rhetorician's rules
> Teach nothing but to name his tools.[2]

DISCUSSION

It sharpens the jokes up. It's the comedian's double-punch – the old one-two: the lead-up to the joke which builds the expectation of laughter and the joke's swift conclusion which releases the laughter you are already half-committed to. In effect, the couplet is carrying Butler to a joke every two lines, and, in a sense, we feel every two rhyming lines as a single unit anyway.

Of course you've got to have the jokes to do this. The couplet will sharpen the jokes: it will not make them. If I can illustrate, here are four more lines from *Hudibras*:

> For he, by geometric scale,
> Could take the size of pots of ale;
> Resolve, by sines and tangents straight,
> If bread or butter wanted weight.[3]

This is funny. If I write

> For Jack, however strong the gale,
> Could keep his dinghy under sail,
> And though sometimes he came home late,
> His patient wife would always wait.

it might be laughable but it isn't funny. Maybe it's working up to a joke, but this isn't it. Butler's couplets are made funny by his fantastic ideas:

> He'd run in debt by disputation,
> And pay with ratiocination.[4]

The couplet is the vehicle for delivering them. And comedy has much to do with delivery, with timing.

Notice how lean the writing is: few adjectives and little packing, even to raise a laugh. This is an enforcement of the eight-syllabled measure that Butler is using. The compensation is the speed of delivery, the instinct of the wisecracking stand-up comic. It's as well to remember here that what Butler says may be true or it may not be. Truth is not necessarily a product of satire or of well-balanced couplets.

Now look at a short extract from Dryden's *Mac Flecknoe* (1682). Dryden is describing Mac Flecknoe, alias the playwright Thomas Shadwell:

> With whate'er gall thou sett'st th yself to write,
> Thy inoffensive Satires never bite.
> In thy felonious heart though venom lies,
> It does but touch thy Irish pen, and dies.
> Thy Genius calls thee not to purchase fame

In keen iambics, but mild anagram:
Leave writing plays, and choose for thy command
Some peaceful province in Acrostic Land.
There thou mayest wings display, and altars raise,
And torture one poor word ten thousand ways.[5]

**What differences and similarities do you notice between these lines
and the ones from *Hudibras*?**

DISCUSSION

Well, there are many similarities. First, an undercutting comedy,
which initially concedes an ability in its subject and then denies it
by applying it to something judged worthless:

Thy Genius calls thee not to purchase fame
In keen iambics, but mild anagram.

Then there is a willingness to fantasticate his examples. Just as
geometry became an aid to drinking in Butler, so acrostics become
a mimic religious rite in Dryden:

There thou mayest wings display, and altars raise,
And torture one poor word ten thousand ways.

The elements of the 'rite' I perceive as being constructed by these
images ('wings', 'altars' and the torturing of words) are all hits at
the style of the Metaphysical poets, particularly George Herbert,
part of whose 'Easter-wings' you have already seen. 'The Altar' is
another of his shaped poems.[6]

    As to the differences, some of them, at least, can be attributed
to Dryden working with ten-syllabled lines rather than with
Butler's octosyllabics. The pace at each stage is slightly slowed.
We are not rushed helter-skelter from idea to idea. Instead, we
savour them. Adjectives appear – 'inoffensive', 'felonious', 'keen',
'mild', 'peaceful', 'poor'. To test the way these adjectives alter
things, here's how the passage might be written in eight-syllabled
lines:

Whatever gall drives thee to write,
Thy Satires ne'er begin to bite.
And in thy heart though venom lies,
It does but touch thy pen and dies.
Thy Genius should not look for fame
In iambics but in anagram.
Leave plays and choose as your command
Some corner in Acrostic Land.
Display thy wings; an altar raise,
Torture one word ten thousand ways.

The effect is obviously much more bare, though no idea has been dropped. But notice the sensitive observation in a phrase like Dryden's 'thou sett'st thyself to write' – the deliberation in the reflexive verb. In eight syllables, those six are too much, and a delicate touch is lost. Perhaps at first sight the adjectives don't seem much, but leave them out and you realize how exactly weighted they are. 'Inoffensive Satires' undercuts everything Shadwell does before it reaches the stage, at the end of the line, of never biting. The 'keen'/'mild' opposition is total and extremely economic of space, but even this has to go in octosyllabics because you have to retain 'iambics' and 'anagram'. Compare Butler's use of 'geometric', 'disputation', 'ratiocination', 'rhetorician' – such technical words use up syllables very fast. Ten syllables gives you that little bit more room. And, lastly, the withering effect of 'peaceful province' becomes a luxury in eight syllables. So much of the colour and nuance must be given up in order to keep the argument going. It becomes a poetry much closer to statement, much less conditioned.

Dryden's last couplet, though, indicates one way in which ten-syllabled lines may produce their own turn of speed. As he moves into his description of Shadwell's potential in Acrostic Land, he develops in a single couplet three ideas: a peacock-like display, the construction of a number of altars, and the torturing of words into acrostic shapes. The twenty syllables he has are just enough to contain all that, disparate as the ideas seem. In fact, one could fancy that Dryden might have been looking to draw the three ideas together in a more coherent and fantastic single-minded rite. 'And altars raise' would then fit more snugly, instead of giving a slight feeling that it is anchored only as a further reference to Herbert.

In my reworking, I kept the ideas, but at the price of losing all the little connective words that keep things from becoming too staccato or chopped. What Butler would have done, I fancy, is not to try to pack the three ideas in the two lines but to fill them out by writing another couplet. With couplets, there's no reason to stop writing them until you've finished what you are going to say. Indeed, in a fast-moving metre like octosyllabics, there's every reason to give each idea its couplet and to keep the couplets going. Here it would give you a chance to increase the fantasy. For example, you could put in an additional reference to the Metaphysical manner – this time to Crashaw's 'The Weeper'[7] – draw a key word from 'Easter-wings', and come up with a much more unified sense of the whole image:

And there may'st thou display thy wings,
Build up thy fanes, weep sacred springs;
For thy thin rites an altar raise,
And torture words ten thousand ways.

Incidentally, you'll notice that merely reducing the pentameters to octosyllabics doesn't make the Dryden sound like Butler. The two poets don't start from the same place and so such a change won't of itself bring them much closer. Their 'voice' is not the same. Part of that difference is, of course, the use of their own favoured metres. The kinds of rhymes they use are different too. Butler's rhymes have a comic potential, or perhaps it is better to say he puts words in comic circumstances. Dryden's are not like that. His rhymes are for the most part universally available. By that, I mean that, if you were given rhymes like 'disputation'/ 'ratiocination', 'scale'/'ale', 'trope'/'ope', 'off'/'cough', the poem you might construct from them is already being steered towards a particular tone. Dryden's rhymes do not commit you like that, except for 'fame'/'anagram' which, notice, was probably a full rhyme in 1682.

There is one other difference that is worth noting in these two ways of handling rhyming couplets. Again, the difference really comes down to the fact that octosyllabics are two syllables shorter than iambic pentameters – and what follows from that. Because the ideas in *Hudibras* are fertile and flow beyond the limits of the couplet, they give rise to uninterrupted sequences such as lines 3 to 6 of the passage first quoted. For the pleasure of quoting a little more, here is the poem's opening sequence of fourteen lines. Its conclusion is held up to the very last line:

When civil fury first grew high,
And men fell out, they knew not why;
When hard words, jealousies, and fears,
Set folks together by the ears,
And made them fight, like mad or drunk,
For Dame Religion as for punk,
Whose honesty they all durst swear for,
Though not a man of them knew wherefore:
When gospel-trumpeter surrounded,
With long-eared rout to battle sounded,
And pulpit, drum ecclesiastic,
Was beat with fist instead of a stick;
Then did Sir Knight abandon dwelling,
And out he rode a-colonelling.[8]

Think of passages you could drop here if you were trying to save space. Would you keep lines 3 to 8, say, or lines 11 to 12? You certainly could shorten it. You would gain space and, perhaps, sharpen the whole thing up. But would you be losing anything? Well, I think so. Sharper it might be, but not so joyous, nor so active and crowded.

For Butler, the couplet naturally gave rise to extension. Can you see how Dryden's more ample lines are much more comfortable as self-contained couplets? Look at the opening of *Mac Flecknoe*:

> All human things are subject to decay,
> And, when Fate summons, monarchs must obey:
> This Flecknoe found, who, like Augustus, young
> Was call'd to empire and had govern'd long:
> In prose and verse was own'd, without dispute
> Through all the realms of non-sense, absolute.[9]

The tendency is towards a sequence of two-line epigrams, each complete, but linked in a progressive sequence both with what precedes and what follows it. This is a tendency, not a necessity, but it is a tendency frequently to be observed in the poem. The technique of stopping at the end of the line (end-stopping), used in conjunction with the couplet, sets up a particular pattern both in the form and in the thought of the poem, and gives great prominence to devices using parallel constructions. A typical couplet would be:

> No Persian carpets spread th'imperial way,
> But scatter'd limbs of mangled poets lay.[10]

This manner reached its height and, it is not foolish to say, its perfection in the writing of Alexander Pope (1688–1744) and is used by him, characteristically, in 'essays' on moral, social and aesthetic questions, handled in a satiric way. Thus in *An Essay on Criticism* he writes:

> 'Tis hard to say, if greater want of skill
> Appear in writing or in judging ill;
> But, of the two, less dangerous is the offence
> To tire our patience, than mislead our sense.
> Some few in that, but numbers err in this,
> Ten censure wrong for one who writes amiss;
> A fool might once himself alone expose,
> Now one in verse makes many more in prose.
> 'Tis with our judgments as our watches, none
> Go just alike, yet each believes his own.[11]

Pope is comparing two types of writing: poetry and criticism. How does the couplet form contribute to his case?

DISCUSSION

The first thing to notice is that it is, in fact, a case: an argument to discriminate between ideas, to win or to lose. It raises an important question on which you could appropriately write a treatise, but the poem has a way of getting to the point quicker than a treatise would. The final couplet of the extract is as succinct an account of the place of subjectivity and relativity in criticism as one could imagine. Its effect, if taken to heart, is to devastate not so much our opinions as the absolute value we are prone to confer on them, especially in these days of quartz judgements.

The couplets, then, are being used to present a case and to present it hard. But, interestingly enough, the final couplet of the sequence is the only instance of an image being used to give substance or colour to the thought. The rest is argument, kept firmly in place by rhyme and parallel rhythms alone. But there is a danger in the way the argument is set up. It is not quite honest in its procedures. Pope starts off by disclaiming a firm position in the question of whether bad poetry or bad criticism is evidence of 'greater want of skill' – it's hard to say, he says. Then he goes on, but one is less dangerous – bad poetry – because it only bores us and doesn't mislead us. From then on the question is firmly decided, with phoney, even if only symbolic, numbers and primitive statistics – 'few in that'; 'numbers . . . in this'; 'ten . . . for . . . one'; 'one . . . many more'. The move is subtle, and we have essentially been deceived by rhythmic sleight-of-hand. The argument, from looking sweetly reasonable, is now merely assertive.

There is one other fault in the argument that is to be ascribed to the pattern, and that is the all-or-nothing case that parallel constructions invite us to accept. In this instance, the worst of poetry's faults is that it tires our patience; the worst of criticism's faults is that it misleads our sense. But could poetry not mislead us too? After all, Pope is asserting a case in 'sense', not simply trying not to bore us. Equally, criticism can 'tire our patience', and how. The effect of parallel expression – if this, then that; if not this, then that – is to set up oppositions that require assumptions of us before we have properly entered into the discussion. And, especially, it requires rather gross simplification in the terms opposed. Of course, poetry, with its emblematizing and symbolizing manner, always involves such simplification, but then poetry does not normally pretend to establish the kind of truth that philosophy, for example, proposes. We look for insight, consolation, celebration, the salvage of feeling more than we do for faultless ideology. Is this implied in Pope's initial contrast? Is that why poetry cannot mislead us, only bore us? Well, it may be, but it is an unpresented assumption, and, in an 'essay on criticism', that is at least dangerous.

A further question. In Chapter 4, I quoted T. S. Eliot's view that 'to have the virtues of good prose is the first and minimum requirement of good poetry'. Do you think Pope's couplets here have 'the virtues of good prose'?

DISCUSSION

Well, certainly, the writing is clear, uncluttered and elegant. It takes upon itself the 'burdens' of prose, engaging the materials of the thesis-writer or the polemicist. It argues a case. But maybe to be too strongly engaged with 'cases' and winning and losing them is not the best thing poetry can do. Perhaps poetry is better concerned not with conclusions but with implying the range of possibility within which conclusions are only temporary marks to be achieved and left behind. To put it another way, poetry is best open-ended, whereas lines like

'Tis with our judgments as our watches, none
Go just alike, yet each believes his own.

are brilliantly closed. Here poetry – metre, image, rhyme, balance – provides the brilliance. Prose requires that a case must be made.

Here, though, we may be guilty of just the fault I am imputing to Pope; the all-or-nothing opposition – poetry gives this, prose gives that. It is more probable that they share qualities and solutions. There are, after all, different kinds of poetry and different uses for it. In the case of the balance in the form of the couplet, balance was a great feature of eighteenth-century prose too. If it was a virtue, it was a virtue of the age, and of the style that went with it. And, while I have been at pains to point out that an oppositional balance in constructing a case has dangers, it would not be true to say that arguments that depend on such balance are necessarily wrong; it is not the rhythm that is wrong: it is what we ask the rhythm to carry that is the problem. Some balances may well be true. But some are inadmissible. And the rhythm, as a rhythm, as paired rhyme, cannot distinguish between the two. It can only be used, compelling the disparate sounds that occupy it into relationship.

This sense of finish, of balanced shape, in the so-called heroic couplet such as Pope was writing, coincided with the ordered, classical bearing which was the mental pattern of the age. In a phrase of Pope's, the world was 'a mighty maze! but not without a plan' – a world more problematic, hence soluble, than it was mysterious.[12] John Keats, in the early nineteenth century, used rhymed couplets to resist just such a view of the world and to project it instead, as both wondrous and fearful. He writes in *Lamia*, with Newton's discoveries in mind:

> Do not all charms fly
> At the mere touch of cold philosophy?
> There was an awful rainbow once in heaven:
> We know her woof, her texture; she is given
> In the dull catalogue of common things.
> Philosophy will clip an Angel's wings,
> Conquer all mysteries by rule and line,
> Empty the haunted air, and gnomèd mine –
> Unweave a rainbow, as it erewhile made
> The tender-personed Lamia melt into a shade.[13]

Plainly, these are rhymed couplets. Are they used, just as Pope's were, to argue a case? And is the couplet itself used differently? Keep in mind any socio-metric pointers to a shift in sensibility here.

DISCUSSION

Keats is arguing just as much as Pope was. His concern is with the effect of scientific explanations of nature on sensibility. The new knowledge unweaves the rainbow. What is prime for Keats in these lines is not the search for objective knowledge and the excitement of its discovery, but the loss of feeling – charms, awe, mystery. These things, Keats would suggest, are a more important reality. No matter that Lamia is an illusory, false presence in the poem, a sorceress. We need our illusions as much as our knowledge.

Keats's use of the couplet to put forward this anti-rational assessment of things should make us wary of identifying metres or privileged poetic structures with particular ideologies. Again, it is a question of what words and arguments fill up the metric. But we could, perhaps, note that Keats does not use the couplet in the closed and balanced way that Pope does. There is far less end-stopping. He does not set up a chain of reasoning, unit by unit, but a single, reiterative, rhetorical sequence. He asks a loaded question ('mere touch' and 'cold' are the loaded words), moving from facts, suitably slanted, using words like 'awful' and its opposite 'dull' to slant them, to an assertion about philosophy and back, finally, to the narrative, to a story that does not seem to bear out Keats's case. Rather, it presents his dilemma: the impossible choice in a world where dull Newtons outface delightful Lamias. The way Keats handles the couplet makes it serve open-endedness and feeling, not closure and a supposed objective truth.

Of course, there was just as much 'feeling' in the eighteenth as in the nineteenth century. It was apt to express itself differently, that's all. Equally, Keats's fellow-romantic, Shelley, was passionately interested in and knowledgeable about science, and involved his knowledge in, for example, *Prometheus Unbound*.

That is probably as far as we can get with the couplet as a point of contrast between the eighteenth and nineteenth centuries, so let's look at some different forms now. First, here are three stanzas from William Cowper's poem 'The Castaway', which was written in 1799. That's as late as it could be in the eighteenth century, admittedly, but the expression is acceptably eighteenth-century. The poem describes the death of a drowning sailor. Cowper had read the story in Anson's *Voyage Round the World* (1748). In the early stanzas of the poem, he recounts the circumstances and presumed feelings of the man as he realizes he is beyond help and must die. Cowper himself was an extreme depressive, often suicidal. Here are the stanzas I would like you to look at.

No poet wept him: but the page
Of narrative sincere,
That tells his name, his worth, his age,
Is wet with Anson's tear.
And tears by bards or heroes shed
Alike immortalize the dead.

I therefore purpose not, or dream,
Descanting on his fate,
To give the melancholy theme
A more enduring date:
But misery still delights to trace
Its semblance in another's case.

No voice divine the storm allay'd,
No light propitious shone;
When, snatch'd from all effectual aid,
We perish'd, each alone:
But I beneath a rougher sea,
And whelm'd in deeper gulphs than he.[14]

Two questions. Is the sailor's despair, as distinct from Cowper's, something observed rather than felt? And how much does your conclusion depend on the tight form of the writing?

DISCUSSION

Well, certainly it's observed. Cowper is not drowning physically, nor are we: nor, indeed, was Anson, the author of the original story that Cowper now tells. But we shouldn't equate observation from a distance with lack of feeling. We know that Anson wept (line 4). We know that Cowper feels. Even if he feels his own griefs more, nonetheless he knows that the sailor also perished alone, and he can give that a personal and therefore intense meaning. Cowper widens the area within which grief operates without displacing the original incident.

As to the second question, our conclusions ought obviously to be derived from the way the poem is written. It's the best evidence we have. And certainly the writing is tight. Cowper wrote hymns, and the first four lines of each of his stanzas parallel exactly the structure of, for example, his celebrated

> God moves in a mysterious way,
>   His wonders to perform;
> He plants his footsteps in the sea,
>   And rides upon the storm.[15]

In the final couplet of each stanza, Cowper is encouraged to a shaped conclusion, which, as we have been noticing, is a dominant characteristic of eighteenth-century uses of rhyming couplets:

> And tears by bards and heroes shed
> Alike immortalize the dead.

Cowper's form then, in its habitual associations – hymns and couplets – in its spareness of line – 8 6 8 6 8 8 – and in its need to reach some sort of interim conclusion every six lines, most fully to exploit the couplet, is well suited by a generalizing tendency which is less a removal from the castaway's predicament than an enhancement of it, giving him common cause with others and making him exemplary. I am suggesting that the formality of the poem elevates the passion at the same time as it keeps it tight. The clue to this is the final couplet:

> But I beneath a rougher sea,
> And whelm'd in deeper gulphs than he.

which seems to remove the poem from its concern with the drowning sailor and makes us ask who is the 'castaway' now, Cowper or the sailor. Cowper may not have laid down his life for another, but he has, insofar as you can in writing a poem, identified himself with another in death. If Cowper sees his own grief as greater, it is because he has countenanced the sailor's grief, invited it in, and it has augmented his own. The 'delight' – strange word – he feels in the preceding stanza is in tracing 'semblance', that is, in seeing that we are alike. Knowing the depths of his own 'gulphs', this is compassion not displacement. Whatever else, we cannot question the intensity of eighteenth-century feeling. And the form does not so much distance it as give it a particular intellectual shape.

To get some idea of the change of sensibility in the crucial early part of the nineteenth century, I would like you to look at these lines from Coleridge's 'This Lime-Tree Bower My Prison'. Some friends are staying with Coleridge, but a domestic accident stops him going for a walk with them.

> Well, they are gone, and here must I remain,
> This lime-tree bower my prison! I have lost
> Beauties and feelings, such as would have been
> Most sweet to my remembrance, even when age
> Had dimm'd mine eyes to blindness! They, meanwhile,
> Friends, whom I never more may meet again,
> On springy heath, along the hill-top edge,
> Wander in gladness, and wind down, perchance,
> To that still roaring dell, of which I told.[16]

What are the characteristics of Coleridge's tone here? How much does that tone depend on the techniques he uses? To decide that, of course, you will have to try to work out what those techniques are. So it is a matter of looking out for rhyme and rhythm and counterpoint, just as we have been doing throughout the book.

DISCUSSION

The tone is conversational, Coleridge, in effect, talking to himself. It moves easily from brooding, a degree of self-dramatization, to a well-presented sense of the natural delights he has accidentally lost. In verse like this, without any constraints of stanza or rhyme, it is possible to register the range of emotions we go through, normally, and as quickly as they occur to us. There is no need, as there often is with a stanza, to pad out the description of a feeling or, alternatively, to constrict it. Blank verse – the name for this rhymeless, stanzaless iambic pentameter – can accurately represent the switchback contours of the mind. Coleridge uses all its resources. The sense runs over the ends of the lines. He counterpoints an iambic rhythm with the rhythm of conversational speech, principally by shifting caesuras from a central position and placing them close to the ends of the lines, most daringly in

Had dimm'd mine eyes to blindness! ‖ They, meanwhile,
Friends, ‖ whom I never more may meet again.

It is all personal to Coleridge, but the reader can feel it very
directly too. The medium is transparent, with enough regulation
not to be amorphous, but not so much as to distract us with its
ingenuities. If art is to conceal art, then this is high art.

At the same time, it does not seem to me that the charge of
feeling in Coleridge is greater than it was in Cowper. It is not any
knowledge we may have of Cowper's life that gives poignancy to
his final stanzas. It is already plain to see, a drowning hand
thrust from a metric ocean. In spite of Cowper's formality and
Coleridge's familiarity, they are closer to one another than any
description of their techniques would suggest. If there is a divide
between eighteenth- and nineteenth-century sensibilities, it is not
primarily in the capacity to feel, to bleed, nor in the capacity of
particular poetic structures to be identified with feeling.

I want you now to look at another example of nineteenth-
century blank verse. It is from Wordsworth's *The Prelude*, and
describes his contending emotions about the French Revolution.
He is in Paris. This is not the Revolution as he had originally
seen it, with 'human nature seeming born again', but as it had
developed after the September massacres in 1792.

> . . . But that night
> I felt most deeply in what world I was,
> What ground I trod on, and what air I breathed.
> High was my room and lonely, near the roof
> Of a large mansion or hotel, a lodge
> That would have pleased me in more quiet times;
> Nor was it wholly without pleasure then.
> With unextinguished taper I kept watch,
> Reading at intervals; the fear gone by
> Pressed on me almost like a fear to come.
> I thought of those September massacres,
> Divided from me by one little month,
> Saw them and touched: the rest was conjured up
> From tragic fictions or true history,
> Remembrances and dim admonishments.
> The horse is taught his manage, and no star
> Of wildest course but treads back his own steps;
> For the spent hurricane the air provides
> As fierce a successor; the tide retreats
> But to return out of its hiding place
> In the great deep; all things have second birth;
> The earthquake is not satisfied at once;
> And in this way I wrought upon myself,
> Until I seemed to hear a voice that cried,

To the whole city, 'Sleep no more'. The trance
Fled with the voice to which it had given birth;
But vainly comments of a calmer mind
Promised soft peace and sweet forgetfulness.
The place, all hushed and silent as it was,
Appeared unfit for the repose of night,
Defenceless as a wood where tigers roam.[17]

I talked of 'contending emotions' in Wordsworth. Is that a
fair description? If so, what is the contention between? At the
back of these questions is, I suppose, a further one. Is there an
underlying couplet-like tune to the way Wordsworth is writing?

DISCUSSION

I think it is a fair description. The contention is between fear and
a longing for peace. This is presented, to some degree, in a balance
of opposites, but, even so, it doesn't go easily to what I am calling
a couplet-like tune. The whole passage seems to invite but not to
achieve tranquillity. It is an uneasy meditation on the revolutionary
times Wordsworth is witness to. And, as with revolution itself, it
has its catastrophic moment – when the voice cries out, Macbeth-
like, 'Sleep no more.' But the rhythms are wave-like, rather than
oppositional. They are so uncoercive in their meditative continuity
that they seem to accommodate anything, even catastrophe, after
which they resume their steady succession, one line upon another.
They are not tuned to oppositions, as couplets are, but to gradations, and to the end of gradations – assimilations. Notice, for
example, how 'the fear gone by . . . a fear to come' looks like an
opposition and is structured as one but is, in fact, a continuity,
pivoting as it does on the word 'Pressed'. The same is true of 'tragic
fictions or true history' which are complementary – both convey-
ing the same message – rather than oppositional. Wordsworth
helps this sense by his following line, a variation in language
register and in rhythm, with its sequence of lightly touched
stresses. The line dissolves opposition in the hesitancies of its
rhythm – 'Remembrances and dim admonishments.'
    Another way in which Wordsworth achieves a rhythmic con-
tinuity is in the sequences he builds, which do not so much
counterpoint with the iambic rhythm as occupy the whole ground
of the lines: 'what world I . . . What ground I . . . what air I . . .'.
Each time, a noun of global implication is metrically linked with
an emphatic 'I' usurping the iambic offbeat. It is a world where
Wordsworth is deep in the heart of things. What happens is
expressly validated by Wordsworth's perception of it – 'I felt', 'I

kept watch', 'I thought', 'Divided from me', 'I seemed to hear' and so on – rather than through our assessing something presented as 'object' both for the poet and for us. This enforces the poet's centrality, which is rhythmically confirmed by the all-including, assimilating voice.

The 'what...I...' sequence prepares us for a series of meditative statements, collateral metaphors or emblems, building to an overall composite metaphor for the secondary revolutionary onslaught, the horror to come. The rhythm of the phrases – 'The horse...', 'no star...but...', 'the air provides...', 'the tide retreats...' and so on – insists on us, not as a counter-rhythm, thrown down over some other rhythm, but by occupying everything that is before us. These images are not observed, but exist only as thoughts in Wordsworth's mind – 'And in this way I wrought upon myself'. As the images are the embodiments of the one mind, so the rhythmic patterns in which the thoughts are embodied establish a single voice. This inclusive Wordsworthian voice arrives through a series of parallels, an aggregation of imagined things, at their simplification: 'all things have second birth'. Such an inclusive simplification is as beguiling and betraying to the intellect as its apparent polar opposite, the heroic couplet, in which, so frequently, one term of the couplet's balance refutes and displaces the other. The mind that can resolve all differences in one will be more at home with the 'mysteries' that Keats celebrates than with the problematic, yet soluble, maze that Pope perceived the world to be. It is the desire to see the world not as a logical if problematic sequence but as a mysterious and inclusive whole that gives the sanction to Wordsworth's sensibility and to romanticism more generally. Planned mazes are out; 'alls' and 'wholes' are in. And 'the growth of a poet's mind' – *The Prelude*'s subtitle – becomes a matter of presumed public interest. After all, that mind is where the whole is first divined and then embodied.

In concluding this exercise in the possibilities of 'sociometrics', it has to be said that Wordsworth's own critical assertions, in his prose writings, are less to do with rhythm than with language. His poetic practice was intent on loosening the grip that strict metre allied to a diction reserved to poetry – 'poetic diction' – had maintained in much eighteenth-century writing. To get away from this, he attempted to write 'the very language of men'.[18] It is the poet as revolutionary, shifting the centre of linguistic and so of social power. But Coleridge makes a very interesting comment on Wordsworth's theory and his practice:

To me it will always remain a singular and noticeable fact; that a theory, which would establish this *lingua communis*, not only as the best, but the only commendable style, should have proceeded from a poet, whose diction, next to that of Shakespeare and Milton, appears to me of all others the most individualised and characteristic.[19]

I have tried to show that Wordsworth's individuality can be gauged in his assimilative rhythms, all his words subsumed in a single voice and vision. The words he chooses to embody this rhythm indicate a shift in the balance of concern in society, revolutionary in France, gradualist in England. Both words and rhythm crucially divide him from eighteenth-century practice. The quietly insisting, firm yet fussy voice in

> High was my room and lonely, near the roof
> Of a large mansion or hotel, a lodge
> That would have pleased me in more quiet times;

is a signal of more than metrical release, both revolutionary and profound.

7. Particularities and Patternings

I have tried in this short book to explain the workings of rhythm and rhyme. Faced with the need to describe precisely an art that is characteristically open-ended, the pedagogue will be tempted to pursue bigger and better systems of description and to divine in those systems, ever more complexly, the ever more unlikely. I have not felt it useful to add, to those already in existence, a new way of describing the means of poetry. Rather, I have tried to suggest that we engage with the words poets have written, as freshly

as possible, almost as if names for what they do had not been
given to us. When names have been needed, I have gone for the
traditional names, used simply. At the back of my mind has been
Ezra Pound's belief that teachers presenting a masterpiece to their
classes should do it almost as if they 'have never seen it before'.[1] I
have gone for simplicity. Complicating the way we talk about
metre and rhyme only compounds the difficulty of the subject. If
it's that complicated, we can easily say, 'Why bother? – We enjoy
the poetry; let's leave it at that.' And so we fail to engage with the
structures at the heart of the poems we are trying to read. I have
tried to keep these structures approachable.

My second aim has been to make them interesting. I find
questions of technique interesting in themselves. If, for example, I
examine closely how Keats handles a metre or hides a rhyme, it
may give me ideas about how to do different but related things.
But this is an interest, an admiration, that not everyone will share.
So, after trying to convey this particular sort of interest, I have
tried to suggest further ways in which technique is interesting. I
have tried to suggest two approaches. First, poetic technique can
be related to wider cultural questions. This is especially to be
detected at historical periods when the structures of poetry change
radically. Second, I have suggested that poetic structures are
intimately related with our own natures and with the nature of the
world we inhabit. And so, what we have been doing as simply as
we can is not so simple after all. In fact, I have been conscious of a
double principle: that no question is so easy that we can neglect to
ask it; that no question is so difficult that we should be tempted to
avoid asking it. In this chapter, I want to follow up and deepen
the terms of discussion that these approaches invite.

In Chapter 4 we looked at Wilfred Owen's use of pararhyme
in his First World War poems. It would be right and easy to talk
about his tremendous technique and so on, but to do so would be
to invite the response 'So what?' But to see the dislocating effect of
pararhyme as conditioned by Owen's experience of war is to see it
more fully. Then the technical question is not just a passing
curiosity. I would like to take the process further. How often did
artists and writers, faced with the conditions in the First World
War, react by using techniques of dislocation? Is there some relationship between Owen's experiments with rhyme and, say, Paul
Nash's devastated watercolour landscapes of the Western Front as
they relate to the traditions of English watercolour landscape
painting? Is Dada another parallel – a zany sanity, incidentally
often purely linguistic in its means, and offered as a response to
the actual insanity soberly commissioned and paraded as good

sense by the nations of the world in the trenches, or, rather, safely behind the lines?[2] Do we, in fact, see such dislocating images operating even before the war, in Cubist painting, for example, or in the music of Schönberg, or in the reappraisal of the surfaces of our behaviour implied in Freud's investigations of dreams? Might, then, the war itself be as much a symptom of some wider cultural shift, already in process in the early twentieth century, and not simply the cause of some of the more graphic evidences of dislocation?

Now, it can be alleged that the jumps involved in such parallels are speculative and illicit and depend on the dubious use of a blanket metaphor like 'dislocation'. Certainly, to introduce such parallels too early into the discussion would risk explaining the known by the unknown. But, then, how much do we know of, say, 'Strange Meeting' anyway?

> Then, as I probed them, one sprang up, and stared
> With piteous recognition in fixed eyes,
> Lifting distressful hands as if to bless.
> And by his smile, I knew that sullen hall,
> By his dead smile I knew we stood in Hell.

To know these lines, the shock of recognition there, we should try all the means we have. All our investigations will be implied in Owen's shifting rhymes: from 'eyes' to 'bless', from 'hall' to 'Hell'.

My second line of approach, in Chapter 2, was to suggest that pattern, such as rhyme and rhythm is, has meaning in itself. By a gradual refinement of the way we describe the means poetry uses, a minimal structure can be isolated. I have often used the term 'algebra' to describe the way a metre relates to the many lines which can fulfil the metre's requirements. At this next point in the discussion, then, we will be seeking a kind of meta-algebra for poetic structures, a pattern going beyond the patterns and giving a single account that will work for them all. And there are many available descriptions of this minimal kind which all structure in the same way: as binary opposition or, viewed another way, binary complementarity. Wordsworth wrote of metre as working through 'similitude in dissimilitude'; Pound saw the arts as attaining 'their effects by using a fixed element and a variable'; the nineteenth-century poet Gerard Manley Hopkins described rhythm as 'likeness tempered with difference', rhyme as 'agreement of sound' with 'a slight disagreement' and suggested that 'all beauty may by a metaphor be called rhyme'.[3]

Two main binary effects have been suggested in this book. One is rhyme, which has been seen as the pattern for all types of sound-relationship. The second is the alternation of degrees of stress, particularly the light/heavy pairing, the iamb, from which I have sought to derive, by reversal and elongation, a number of other possible metres operating in English verse between the sixteenth century and now. It's important to see that pairs of rhymes and alternations of stresses are, in essence, at the meta-level, the same poetic feature. In any particular instance, we obviously need to discriminate between the rhymes of a sonnet and the rhythm of an iambic pentameter or whatever. But all are, in fact, simply specialized aspects of the structure of relationships that poets set up in their poems. A useful clue to this convergence is in fourteenth-century alliterative verse practice, where a sound-relationship – alliteration – is used as a device to identify rhythmic structure.

In his book *The Founding of English Metre*, John Thompson writes:

> Metre is made by abstracting from speech one of [its] essential features and ordering this into a pattern. The pattern is an imitation of the patterns that the feature makes in speech, a sort of formalizing of these patterns. Actually the metrical pattern represents not only the one feature it is based on but all the essential features of the language. And in organizing these into its abstract patterns, metre follows the principles of our language with the utmost precision.[4]

Iambic metre, he suggests, has 'dominated English verse because it provides the best symbolic model of our language'.[5] Clearly, I have been presenting a similar view, but I would want to modify it substantially in two ways.

First, Thompson's position seems to imply that language is, at its heart, self-regarding, its symbolic heart symbolizing itself. I do not believe that language is like this. Since Adam named the animals, language has always been outgoing. It goes outside itself to possess things certainly, but always to help realize them. We name to love. In Yeats's words, we

> ... murmur name upon name,
> As a mother names her child
> When sleep at last has come
> On limbs that had run wild.[6]

The Beat poet Allen Ginsberg sees at the heart of creation 'the gay Creator [who] dances on his own body in Eternity',[7] and there may be something in that; but other traditions have God's creative act of love giving birth to independently-willed beings, intimate others. So it must be with language, which, even at its most arcane and esoteric, is made to communicate, to connect not with

itself but with life, other lives. If this is the perceived case with
language, it must be as fully true of the element at the heart of the
language's structure, the rhythmic unit which is its epitome.

But there must be another reservation. What about all the
poetry which is not iambic or iambic-derived, which is to say
most twentieth-century and most medieval poetry? The thrust
of Thompson's argument is that the iambic metrical pattern
becomes a sort of linguistic universal corresponding to the English
language, of which each poem is a particular instance. But the
chronologically non-iambic extremes of, say, *Piers Plowman* and
Four Quartets, both undoubtedly poems in the English language,
would indicate that there are non-iambic particular instances. To
what linguistic universal do they relate? In this respect, then,
Thompson's model is again insufficient to the case I am pursuing –
and which I feel it is necessary to pursue – insofar as it fails
to accommodate all instances of non-iambic poems into his
symbolic model of the English language, the language to which
they manifestly belong. However, the impulse behind his case – to
subsume as many particular instances as possible under the one
symbolic pattern of which they are, therefore, expressions – seems
to me right. By such means, a poem's rhythm is not to be seen as
an incidental embellishment or a factor only in our description of
that poem. Rather, the rhythm is at the heart of the poem's
meaning, the condition of its being. Is it possible that the case
could, in fact, be widened?

Could it be that the tendency of things in general to permit
our describing them in terms of such patterns and sets of relationships is, in fact, the means by which we recognize the way those
things exist – the way things are, and not simply the way we
describe them? I say this because the terms I have introduced
here – 'particular' and 'universal' – are the ones traditionally
used in discussing the relationship between things and the general
categories to which they may be assigned. A 'horse' is a particular,
'horseness' the universal of which the horse is an instance. This
distinction, in turn, raises a whole series of problems, mostly
insoluble. It is sufficient to say here that a universal is not a
generalized description, abstracted from many particular instances,
but rather the sum of all possible particular instances, much as the
meaning of a poem can be said to be the sum of all the possible
readings of that poem. A poem, in such an account, provides the
potentially very useful example – to speculative thinking – of a
particular which is its own universal. The medieval philosopher
Duns Scotus sought to intervene in the question of universals with
an idea which, I think, has some kinship with this line of thought.

He had a theory of the 'thisness' – *haecceitas* – of things: that everything was characterized by its 'thisness'.[8] In this way, what gave universality to things was that they all enjoyed *haecceitas*, thisness, indeed particularity.

Gerard Manley Hopkins was much taken by Scotus's ideas. In his turn, he sought to locate what he called the 'inscape' of things. 'Inscaping' was not an impressionistic attempt to seize the soul of something, vapidly conceived, but a rigorous application of the mind to the deep, particularizing structure of an object. This structure had to do with pattern. To stay with horses, in his journal for 6 April 1874, Hopkins wrote that he

> caught that inscape in the horse that you see in the pediment especially and other basreliefs of the Parthenon and even which Sophocles had felt and expresses in two choruses of the *Oedipus Coloneus* running on the likeness of a horse to a breaker, a wave of the sea curling over. I looked at the groin or the flank and saw how the set of the hair symmetrically flowed outwards from it to all parts of the body, so that, following that one may inscape the whole beast very simply.[9]

Recognition of the particularity of things, according to Hopkins, is through their patterning, a created rhythm in the thing itself. But that pattern not only connects the parts of the horse. It connects with artistic visualizations of other horses, in the Parthenon and in Sophocles. And it connects with elements in nature, the wave. For the Christian Hopkins, the deep structure of things was completed in God, where their particularities are not lost but fulfilled. As he put it

> Give beauty back, beauty, beauty, beauty, back to God,
>   beauty's self and beauty's giver.[10]

In my pursuit of the meaning of poetic structures, I'm not suggesting that, if you believe in the iambic pentameter, you will discover the secrets of the universe. But I do wish, at least, to suggest that the crucial structural devices that poetry embodies connect with something beyond the structures of language itself.

To complete my jigsaw, I want to add one more element to this account of poetic structure. To pattern and binary alternation I want to add movement. We looked at William Carlos Williams's methods in Chapter 4. In his poem 'The Wind Increases', he writes:

> Good Christ what is
> a poet – if any
>   exists?

```
a man
whose words will
        bite
                their way
home – being actual
having the form
                of motion
At each twigtip
new
upon the tortured
body of thought
        gripping
the ground
a way
        to the last leaftip[11]
```

'The form of motion' is established in the poem's rocking, breathing structures. This rhythmic physicality serves to remind us of how much in our physical life is rhythmic. All our unconscious processes are rhythmic – the circulation of the blood, our breathing and so on. Equally, rhythmic repetition helps to suspend or allay our consciousness in religious chant, hypnosis, drumming, disco, rock concerts and so on, and, arguably, helps to open us up to other types of experience beyond our consciousness.

I want to suggest, then, that the playing off of one element against another in binary alternation results in a constant pattern which is perpetually in movement. The relaxation of the binary, as in modern irregular metres, only stretches out the terms – the period, the intervals – of the alternation. Alternation between degrees of stress is still there, and therefore rhythm, but more subtly interspersed. Similarly with the medieval pre-iambic metres. Alternation between degrees of stress is still at work. Only its periods and its decisiveness in shaping the verse line are different. All poetic structures coalesce around the same algebraic account, a combination of alternation in time and stress, forming a pattern, perpetually in movement. The 'meaning' of rhythm and rhyme, and all other of the netting effects in poetry, by however tight or slack a recurrence it is achieved, is constant. All the devices, however technically we may attempt to assess them, are means of accommodating particular insights and events to a pattern of permanence, but in such a way that the movement, the constant play of the elements employed, is preserved. We have a sense of the 'being' of the poem – its patterned essence – but also of its 'becoming', its realization and its potential realizations, always different as we read and re-read it and come across different 'performances' of it. We consciously attend to the fluid performance and unconsciously absorb the patterned essence.[12]

But, before that, somebody must write the poem. To end, then, here is an account of the Russian poet Mayakovsky at work:

> I walk about, gesticulating, mumbling still almost without words, now shortening my steps in order not to impede my mumbling, now mumbling more quickly in time to my steps.
>
> Thus is the rhythm hewn and shaped – the rhythm which is the basis of all poetic work and which goes through it like a rumble. Gradually from this rumbling one begins to squeeze out single words ... First and most frequently, the main word becomes apparent – the main word which characterizes the meaning of the verse or the word which is to be rhymed. The remaining words come and arrange themselves in relation to the main one.[13]

This is how one particular poet details the pursuit of structure: a search for rhythm, rhyme and word. Mayakovsky's account sets out, in the single figure of the poet at work, the fixity, the variation and the movement that all poets court and all poems contain.

Glossary

assonance   Correspondence of vowels but not consonants; for example, 'jade'/'pain'. Used regularly at the ends of verse lines, it produces vowel, or assonantal rhyme.

ballad   A traditional and popular form, often narrative and using a four-line stanza, the second and fourth lines rhyming and the lines approximating syllabically to 8 6 8 6. Literary imitations of the form are called literary ballads.

blank verse   Unrhymed iambic pentameter used characteristically in drama by Shakespeare, and as an epic measure by Milton.

cadence   A falling or rising in the movement of the speaking or singing voice, especially towards a line-end or pause. The use of cadences in liturgical plain chant may have parallels in some medieval poetry, including Chaucer's. There are similar effects in the work of Allen Ginsberg, the twentieth-century American Beat poet, in his case influenced by Hebrew chant.

consonance   Correspondence of consonants but not vowels; for example, 'Jane'/'join'. Used regularly at the ends of lines, it produces consonantal rhyme, also called pararhyme or half-rhyme.

enjambement   Carrying the sense of a verse line beyond the end of the line and into the next one. The opposite of end-stopping.

free verse   Verse which is governed by the poet's personal sense of rhythm and the requirements of the poem rather than by any approximation to a recurring metre. Although the terms are often used as if they were interchangeable, free verse is not quite the same as the French *vers libre*, which is more a slackening of the highly specific rules of classical French verse while maintaining regular though non-classical rhythms.

haiku   A seventeen-syllable poem with three lines (5 7 5). It is a highly concentrated and economic form, originally Japanese, but also much used in twentieth-century Western poetry.

heroic couplet   Two rhyming lines in iambic pentameter, characteristically used by Dryden and Pope.

metre   A recurrent pattern in verse, established by the regular placing or counting of stress, syllable or sound. Metre is often perceived as somehow rigid and mechanical; as distinct from rhythm, thought of as 'flow'. But in reality metre is simply the means by which we most readily recognize and, indeed, create rhythm and may be as rigid or as fluid as we like to make it.

open form   Verse in which the phrases of the poem are placed on the page without reference to a fixed left-hand margin and in which the length of the poetic unit is determined by the assumed length of the poet's breath. The theory of open form was developed by the American poet Charles Olson, teacher at Black Mountain College, North Carolina. See his book *Projective Verse* (1950).

ottava rima   A stanza, Italian in origin, of eight eleven-syllabled lines, rhyming ABABABCC, used brilliantly by Byron in *Don Juan*, but modified to iambic pentameter to suit the conditions of English.

quatrain   A four-line stanza.

rhyme royal   A stanza of seven ten-syllabled lines, rhyming ABABBCC, much used by Chaucer.

Spenserian stanza   The stanza used in Spenser's *The Faerie Queene*, nine iambic lines rhyming ABABBCBCC, in which the first eight lines have ten syllables each, the last twelve syllables.

stanza   A recurring pattern of verse lines. In any given poem, the number of lines used as a repeating unit, its constant rhyme-scheme and metre will define the particular stanza. Stanzas are used to give recurrent local shape and articulation to the varied events and ideas that the poem presents.

stress   The emphasis given to a word as it is spoken. Linguisticians distinguish several degrees of stress, as many as five in some accounts. For the purposes of establishing the scansion of English poetry, however, it is best to work with only two degrees of stress: light and heavy. Linguistically speaking this is only a rule of thumb, but, allied with common sense, it works. The common sense is in deploying differential weighting in the stresses, to clarify meaning and to counterpoint the basic verse rhythm with a rhythm that is more like that of conversation.

syllable   Linguistically this is hard to define, since definition implies a supposed singularity of utterance, yet it is often one involving complex sound relationships. For poets, a rule of thumb generally operates here too: 'peat' is one syllable, 'Peter' two, and 'Peterloo' three.

syllabics   A modern type of verse where the lines are determined in their length by syllable count alone, the number of syllables being determined by the poet for the particular poem.

terza rima   The form, very difficult in English, used by Dante for his *Divine Comedy*. The lines are set in stanzas of three eleven-syllabled lines, iambic with an added final syllable. The middle line of each three-line stanza rhymes with the first and third lines of the next stanza. Many poets have tried to render the stanza in English, but it is not easy, both because there are fewer rhymes in English than in Italian and because English feminine rhymes (the added final syllable) are even less common. In English, therefore, poets usually modify its strict requirements as to rhyme and/or syllable count. See, for example, T. S. Eliot, *Four Quartets*, 'Little Gidding' II, lines 25ff., and Seamus Heaney, 'Station Island' XII.

Notes

Chapter 1

1 Morris Halle and Samuel Jay Kayser, quoted in Donald C. Freeman (ed.), *Linguistics and Literary Style* (New York, Holt, Rinehart and Winston, 1970), p. 381.

2 Roman Jakobson, 'Linguistics and Poetics', in T. Sebeok (ed.), *Style in Language* (Cambridge, MA, MIT Press, 1960), p. 358.

3 William Wordsworth, 'Resolution and Independence'; full text in John Wain (ed.), *The Oxford Anthology of English Poetry* ['*OAEP*'] (Oxford, Oxford University Press, 1990), vol. II, pp. 58–62.

4 Desmond Graham, *Introduction to Poetry* (London, Oxford University Press, 1968), p. 124.

5 This example, with Hamer's scansion, is quoted in John Thompson, *The Founding of English Metre* (London, Routledge & Kegan Paul, 1966), p. 134.

6 Thompson, *The Founding of English Metre*, p. 137. The suggested scansion is my own.

7 Wain, *OAEP*, vol. II, p. 431. There are further extracts on pp. 431–7.

8 Ibid., vol. II, pp. 416 and 418. Full text on pp. 416–19.

9 Ibid., vol. I, p. 200. The lines all end with long syllables, often in extended sequences (lines 1 and 2). Line 6 has nine longs and only one short ('tyr-'). But Donne breaks into these measured sequences with little clusters of shorts ('imagin'd', 'trumpets', 'infinit-[ies]', 'from death', 'flood did'). These sudden variations are electrifying, mixing awe and grandeur with alarm and finality, precisely to match the subject, the Last Judgement. It must, though, be stressed that this is a matter of quantity being used to reinforce the meanings in the words Donne has chosen to put in sequence. The overall pace of the passage has been deliberately slowed by the long quantities. This matches the syntax, a single sentence slowly building through all eight lines. Even the short vowels are often used in such a way that you can't read them quickly ('from death', 'flood did').

10 James Gibson (ed.), *The Complete Poems of Thomas Hardy* (London, Macmillan, 1976), pp. 495–6.

11 The term is originally French, coming either from the use of such a line by the medieval French poet Alexandre Paris or from its use in a

number of medieval French poems about Alexander the Great.

12 The first two lines rhyme with the last two, but from the beginnings to the ends of the lines ('Avoid'/'void'; 'Do'/'too'; 'men'/'Then'; 'it'/ 'Is'). There's a bit of liberty there, but I was trying to hide them. These lines, then, are ten-syllabled couplets of a peculiar kind. Putting rhymes at the beginning as well as the ends of lines helps to avoid writing iambic, since rhymes often take heavy stress. But my main device for avoiding iambic was in the body of the poem. The ten-line mid-section has lines of seven syllables alternating with a variable line, but, in practice, always eight or nine syllables. Eight of the ten lines have an odd number of syllables, which again works against iambic. The seven-syllabled line makes you very sparing with adjectives which hold up action. The mixture of line-lengths should help vary your rhythms, because the thought-units will also vary. Finally, I'm not sure I was concerned with this, but there are fourteen lines here, so it could be that this is some sort of distant cousin to a sonnet. So much for the techniques. The meaning, too, is 'concealed', in the subtitle 'Visitation', which refers to Luke 1:39–45.

Chapter 2

1 The terms 'cooked' and 'raw' are used by the French anthropologist Claude Lévi-Strauss. The first volume of his *Mythologiques* is called *Le Cru et le Cuit* (1964). Cooking turns nature into culture, the 'raw' into the 'cooked'.

2 Patrick Heron, *The Changing Forms of Art* (London, Routledge & Kegan Paul, 1955), pp. 52–65. Where Heron quotes Bernard Leach directly, he is referring to Leach's *A Potter's Portfolio*.

3 Ibid., p. 52.

4 Ibid., p. 52.

5 Ibid., pp. 57–8.

6 Ibid., p. 59.

7 Ibid., p. 64.

8 Ibid., p. 64.

9 Ibid., p. 65.

10 Wallace Stevens, *The Necessary Angel: Essays on Reality and the Imagination* (London, Faber and Faber, 1960), p. 160.

11 Wallace Stevens, *The Collected Poems of Wallace Stevens* (London, Faber and Faber, 1955), p. 76.

12 T. S. Eliot, *Collected Poems 1909–1962* (London, Faber and Faber, 1963), p. 194.

13 William Shakespeare, *The Winter's Tale*, I.ii.120–7.

14 Robert Herrick, 'To the Virgins, To Make Much of Time', in Wain, *OAEP*, vol. I, p. 234.

15 Eliot, *Collected Poems 1909–1962*, p. 67. *The Waste Land* is also in Wain, *OAEP*, vol. II, pp. 620–31.

16 Wain, *OAEP*, vol. II, pp. 268–9. I have adopted a different punctuation in the final two lines for the sake of a more intelligible meaning. The change does not affect any of the questions of rhythm and rhyme that will be discussed.

Chapter 3

1 Hyder Edward Rollins (ed.), *The Letters of John Keats 1814–1821* (Cambridge, Cambridge University Press, 1958), vol. II, p. 323, letter of 16 August 1820.
2 Geoffrey N. Leech, *A Linguistic Guide to English Poetry* (London, Longman, 1969), pp. 56–7.
3 R. Murray Schafer (ed.), *Ezra Pound and Music: The Complete Criticism* (London, Faber and Faber, 1978), p. 289.
4 Robert Browning, *The Poems*, ed. John Pettigrew, completed Thomas J. Collins (Harmondsworth, Penguin Books, 1981), vol. 1, p. 739.
5 H. M. Margoliouth (ed.), *The Poems and Letters of Andrew Marvell* (Oxford, Clarendon Press, 2nd ed., 1967), vol. 1, p. 36.
6 William Makepeace Thackeray, 'The Sorrows of Werther', in Michael Roberts (ed.), *The Faber Book of Comic Verse* (London, Faber and Faber, 1942), p. 119.
7 Derek Attridge, *The Rhythms of English Poetry* (London, Longman, 1982), p. 98. The lines from Auden are part of his poem 'Victor'.
8 On the influence of Hebrew poetry on English poetry in the eighteenth and nineteenth centuries, see Murray Roston, *Prophet and Poet: The Bible and the Growth of Romanticism* (London, Faber and Faber), 1965.
9 Wain, *OAEP*, vol. II, p. 162.
10 Ibid., vol. II, p. 297.
11 Ibid., vol. II, p. 208.
12 Francis Sylvester Mahony (known as Father Prout), in Brendan Kennelly (ed.), *The Penguin Book of Irish Verse* (Harmondsworth, Penguin Books, 1970), p. 186. Wain, *OAEP*, also prints a version of the poem (vol. II, p. 337).

Chapter 4

1 See Peter Ackroyd, *T. S. Eliot* (London, Hamish Hamilton, 1984), p. 279.
2 T. S. Eliot, *Selected Prose*, ed. John Hayward (London, Penguin Books, 1953), pp. 165–6. The quotation is from Eliot's Introductory Essay to Johnson's *London: A Poem* and *The Vanity of Human Wishes*, 1930.
3 Ezra Pound, *Make it New* (London, Faber and Faber, 1934).
4 Walt Whitman, *The Complete Poems*, ed. Francis Murphy (Harmondsworth, Penguin Books, 1975), p. 87. The phrases are from 'Song of Myself'.
5 Ibid., p. 124.
6 Ezra Pound, *ABC of Reading* (London, Faber and Faber, 1951) contains a 'Treatise on Metre', pp. 197–206. T. S. Eliot's introduction to Ezra Pound, *Selected Poems* (London, Faber and Faber, 1959) is generally enlightening. For Williams, see Charles Tomlinson's introduction to William Carlos Williams, *Selected Poems* (Harmondsworth, Penguin Books, 1976) and Mike Weaver, *William Carlos Williams: The American Background* (Cambridge, Cambridge University Press, 1971), especially Chapter 5, 'An American Measure', pp. 65–88.

7 *In the American Grain* is the title of a book by Williams, published in 1925.
8 William Carlos Williams, *The Collected Poems of William Carlos Williams*, ed. Christopher MacGowan (New York, New Directions Publishing, 1991), vol. II (1939–62), p. 257.
9 William Carlos Williams, *Paterson, Books I–V* (London, MacGibbon & Kee, 1964), p. 10.
10 William Carlos Williams, 'The Poem as a Field of Action' (1948). This talk, given at the University of Washington, is readily available in Ronald Gottesman *et al.* (eds.), *The Norton Anthology of American Literature* (New York, W. W. Norton and Company, 1979), vol. II, pp. 1455–64. The quotation is on p. 1460.
11 Ibid., p. 1458.
12 Wain, *OAEP*, vol. II, p. 649. Wain also prints Owen's 'Insensibility' and 'Miners', which use similar rhymes.
13 Pound, *ABC of Reading*, p. 32.

Chapter 5

1 I am using this coinage to mean the study of metre in its relation to the structures of society. It's not to be confused with 'sociometry', the study of sociological relationships, especially of preferences, within social groups.
2 Donald B. Sands (ed.), *Middle English Verse Romances* (Exeter, University of Exeter Press, 1986), pp. 185–200.
3 Ibid., *Sir Orfeo*, lines 325–44. Words that might be a problem are 'sighe' – saw; 'real' – royal; 'degiselich' – wonderful; 'diche' – moat; 'vousour' – vaulting; 'avowed' – decorated; 'aumal' – enamel; 'wones' – halls.
4 Thomas C. Rumble (ed.), *The Breton Lays in Middle English* (Detroit, Wayne State University Press, 1965), p. 218.
5 William Langland, *Piers Plowman*, ed. Elizabeth Salter and Derek Pearsall (London, Edward Arnold, 1967) is a convenient selection.
6 Ibid., p. 153. 'wolleward' – dressed in rough wool; 'recheles renke' – man without a care; 'yede' – went; 'lorel' – layabout; 'lened' – lay down; 'lenten' – springtime; 'gurles' – children; 'by orgene' – in harmony; 'botles' – without shoes.
7 I have taken these lines from *The Pardoner's Tale*, as transcribed from the Hengwrt MS, from James G. Southworth, *The Prosody of Chaucer and His Followers* (Oxford, Basil Blackwell, 1962), p. 84.
8 Ian Robinson, *Chaucer's Prosody: A Study of the Middle English Verse Tradition* (Cambridge, Cambridge University Press, 1971), p. 153.
9 See Charles Muscatine, *Chaucer and the French Tradition: A Study in Style and Meaning* (Berkeley and Los Angeles, University of California Press, 1957).
10 Kenneth Muir (ed.), *Collected Poems of Sir Thomas Wyatt* (London, Routledge & Kegan Paul, 1949), p. 28.
11 *Songes and Sonettes (Tottel's Miscellany)*, 1557 (Leeds, A Scolar Press Facsimile, The Scolar Press, 1966). Pages unnumbered.

12 Wain, *OAEP*, vol. I, p. 43.
13 Ibid., vol. I, p. 201.
14 Schafer, *Ezra Pound and Music: The Complete Criticism*, p. 12.
15 Charles Causley, *Collected Poems 1951–1975* (London, Macmillan, 1975), p. 69.
16 As printed in *Collected Poems*, the sonnet has a subtitle – 'From a Normandy crucifix of 1632' – which lessens, but does not dispel, the riddling.
17 Jean-Paul Sartre, *Existentialism and Humanism*, 1946. Quoted in Richard Ellmann and Charles Feidelson Jr. (eds.), *The Modern Tradition: Backgrounds of Modern Literature* (New York, Oxford University Press, 1965), p. 837.
18 See Henry John Chaytor, *From Script to Print: An Introduction to Medieval Vernacular Literature* (Cambridge, Heffer, 1945).
19 F. E. Hutchinson (ed.), *The Works of George Herbert* (Oxford, Clarendon Press, 1941), p. 43.
20 For a well-illustrated survey of the field, see Christopher de Hamel, *A History of Illuminated Manuscripts* (Oxford, Phaidon Press, 1986).
21 Wain, *OAEP*, vol. I, p. 167. The lines are from Sonnets 55 and 60.

Chapter 6

1 See, for example, W. Jackson Bate, *From Classic to Romantic: Premises of Taste in Eighteenth-Century England* (New York, Harper & Row, 1946).
2 Wain, *OAEP*, vol. I, p. 342.
3 Ibid., vol. I, p. 343.
4 Ibid., vol. I, p. 342.
5 Ibid., vol. I, p. 419.
6 Hutchinson, *The Works of George Herbert*, p. 26.
7 Richard Crashaw in L. C. Martin (ed.), *The Poems, English, Latin and Greek of Richard Crashaw* (Oxford, Clarendon Press, 2nd ed., 1957), pp. 79–83.
8 Wain, *OAEP*, vol. I, p. 340.
9 Ibid., vol. I, p. 414.
10 Ibid., vol. I, p. 417.
11 Ibid., vol. I, p. 474.
12 Alexander Pope, *Essay on Man*, 1.6.
13 John Keats, *The Complete Poems*, ed. John Barnard (Harmondsworth, Penguin Books, 1973), p. 431.
14 H. S. Milford (ed.), *Cowper: Poetical Works* (London, Oxford University Press, 1934; 4th ed., corrections and additions by Norma Russell), p. 432.
15 Ibid., p. 455.
16 Wain, *OAEP*, vol. II, p. 130.
17 William Wordsworth, *The Prelude*, ed. E. de Selincourt (Oxford, Oxford University Press, 1926), pp. 369–71. The lines are from the 1850 version of *The Prelude*. The rather different version printed by Wain, *OAEP*, vol. II, p. 81 is from 1805 and is also printed by Selincourt.

18 Preface to *The Lyrical Ballads*, 1800, 1802, in W. J. B. Owen (ed.), *Wordsworth's Literary Criticism* (London, Routledge & Kegan Paul, 1974), p. 74.

19 Samuel Taylor Coleridge, *Biographia Literaria*, ed. Arthur Symons (London, Dent, 1906; reprinted 1930), p. 218.

Chapter 7

1 Pound, *ABC of Reading*, p. 86.

2 See Ronald Tamplin (ed.), *The Arts: A History of Expression in the Twentieth Century* (London, Harrap, 1991), where Nash and Dada are both illustrated, in the wider context of the First World War.

3 Wordsworth in Owen, *Wordsworth's Literary Criticism*, p. 85. Pound, *ABC of Reading*, p. 201. Hopkins in Humphrey House (ed.), completed Graham Storey, *The Journals and Papers of Gerard Manley Hopkins* (London, Oxford University Press, 1959), pp. 101–2.

4 Thompson, *The Founding of English Metre*, p. 11.

5 Ibid., p. 12.

6 Wain, *OAEP*, vol. II, p. 576.

7 Allen Ginsberg, 'Notes Written on Finally Recording *Howl*', *Evergreen Review* (1959), vol. 3, no. 10, p. 135.

8 See, for instance, the entry 'Duns Scotus' in Antony Flew (ed.), *A Dictionary of Philosophy* (London, Pan Books and Macmillan, 1979).

9 House (ed.), *The Journals and Papers of Gerard Manley Hopkins*, pp. 241–2.

10 W. H. Gardner (ed.), *The Poems of Gerard Manley Hopkins* (Oxford, Oxford University Press, 1956), p. 98. Wain prints a good selection of Hopkins.

11 Gottesman (ed.), *The Norton Anthology of American Literature*, vol. II, p. 1447.

12 See the entry 'Actuality and potentiality' in Flew, *A Dictionary of Philosophy*. There is greater detail in Maurice de Wulf, *An Introduction to Scholastic Philosophy*, trans. P. Coffey (New York, Dover Publications, 1956; first published 1903), pp. 98ff. De Wulf writes (p. 99), '... being is not a something that is changeless and merely static: it must be studied not merely in its state of repose but also in its inception or *becoming*, in its evolution or change (in its *fieri* as well as in its *esse*).'

13 Quoted from Sergei M. Eisenstein, *The Psychology of Composition*, trans. and ed. Alan Upchurch (London, Methuen, 1988), p. 48.

Suggestions for Further Reading

Derek Attridge, *The Rhythms of English Poetry* (London, Longman, 1982). Very thorough and well set out in reviewing a variety of approaches to rhythm, but, like most linguistic approaches, overcomplex.

R. F. Brewer, *Orthometry, The Art of Versification and the Technicalities of Poetry* (Edinburgh, John Grant, 1928). A useful old-fashioned handbook, good to have around.

Aaron Copland, *Music and Imagination* (New York, Mentor Books, 1959).

Jonathan Culler, *Structuralist Poetics: Structuralism, Linguistics and the Study of Literature* (London, Routledge & Kegan Paul, 1975).

C. Day-Lewis, *Poetry for You* (Oxford, Basil Blackwell, 1944). A wise and simple book by a poet: intended for children; recommended to linguisticians.

Denis Donoghue, *The Third Voice: Modern British and American Verse Drama* (Princeton, Princeton University Press, 1959). Excellent throughout, but especially to the point here on T. S. Eliot's dramatic verse-line.

Sergei M. Eisenstein, ed. and trans. Alan Upchurch, *The Psychology of Composition* (London, Methuen, 1988). Russian film-maker with a lot of useful things to say about rhythm in art and life.

T. S. Eliot, *Selected Prose*, ed. John Hayward (London, Penguin Books, 1953). Hayward's selection conveniently gathers a number of Eliot's most important discussions of metrical questions.

Ruth Finnegan, *Oral Poetry, its Nature, Significance and Social Context* (Cambridge, Cambridge University Press, 1977). Comprehensive and extremely useful about the particularities of the oral tradition.

Donald C. Freeman (ed.), *Linguistics and Literary Style* (New York, Holt, Rinehart and Winston, 1970).

Paul Fussell, *Poetic Meter and Poetic Form* (New York, Random House, 1965). A useful book.

Paul Fussell, *Theory of Prosody in Eighteenth-Century England* (Hamden, Connecticut, Archon Books, 1966). Specialized and very informative.

G. P. Goold, *Catullus* (London, Duckworth, 1983). Explains quantity in classical verse very clearly.

Desmond Graham, *Introduction to Poetry* (London, Oxford University Press, 1968). A book of great directness and clarity.

Patrick Heron, *The Changing Forms of Art* (London, Routledge & Kegan Paul, 1955).

Ottó Károlyi, *Introducing Music* (Harmondsworth, Penguin Books, 1965).

J. B. Leishman. *Translating Horace* (Oxford, Bruno Cassirer, 1956). Offers a lively account of quantity.

Ezra Pound, *ABC of Reading* (London, Faber and Faber, 1951). If I were recommending a single book, this would be it.

James Reeves, *Understanding Poetry* (London, Heinemann, 1965). An accessible account.

Philip Davies Roberts, *How Poetry Works: The Elements of English Poetry* (Harmondsworth, Penguin Books, 1986). Contains a lot of good sense, while using a system of laying out a poem called stress-column alignment which seems to me more confusing than revealing.

Ian Robinson, *Chaucer's Prosody: A Study of the Middle English Verse Tradition* (Cambridge, Cambridge University Press, 1971).

T. Sebeok (ed.), *Style in Language* (Cambridge, MA, MIT Press, 1960). Contains Roman Jakobson's 'Linguistics and Poetics'.

Igor Stravinsky, *Poetics of Music in the Form of Six Lessons* (New York, Vintage Books, 1947).

Robert Swann and Frank Sidgwick, *The Making of Verse: A Guide to English Metres* (London, Sidgwick and Jackson, 1934).

John Thompson, *The Founding of English Metre* (London, Routledge & Kegan Paul, 1966).

Lev Semenovich Vygotsky, *The Psychology of Art* (Cambridge, MA, MIT Press, 1971). A book of great general interest which contains some important specific comments on rhythm.

Index